TO CORINTH WITH LOVE

The vital relevance today of
Paul's advice to the
Corinthian church

Michael Green

HODDER AND STOUGHTON
LONDON SYDNEY AUCKLAND TORONTO

British Library Cataloguing in Publication Data

Green, Michael, *1930–*
  To Corinth with love: contemporary issues in
  the light of Paul's letters to Corinth.
  1. Bible. N.T. Corinthians
  2. Church—Biblical teaching
  I. Title
  227'.2'06   BS2675.5

ISBN 0 340 28226 6

TO CORINTH WITH LOVE

For those who have sat with me
at the feet of St Paul
in
St John's College, Nottingham,
Regent College, Vancouver,
and
St Aldate's Church, Oxford

CONTENTS

CHAPTER ONE

A LOVE AFFAIR –
WITH PROBLEMS

The Corinthian church was founded by St Paul some twenty years after the resurrection of Jesus Christ. It was a dynamic – and chaotic – church which he loved with passion and exasperation. We have an extended account of its foundation in Acts 18, and two of the longest letters in the New Testament, 1 and 2 Corinthians, are addressed to it.

Corinth has an enormous amount to say to our contemporary church situation. That is why I have chosen to write on it. Those from solid main-line churches may be challenged afresh by the vitality and spiritual gifts of the Corinthian congregation, and may be moved to re-examine some long-standing assumptions about church life which find no basis here. Those from the younger churches and the house-church movement where spiritual gifts are very much to the fore may well find here that they have something to learn from the way in which Paul handled many problems at Corinth with a curiously modern ring to them, yet without inhibiting vitality or compromising truth and balance.

There are, in any case, many advantages in studying a substantial and homogeneous collection of writings such as the Corinthian correspondence. It is undeniably Pauline, for one thing, though our two letters may originally have been three or even four letters, in whole or in part. It gives us a superb view of Paul the church planter and pastor using his theology not for its own sake but in the service of the church. The spread of abuses and problems at Corinth enables us to share the apostle's perspective on a large number of issues of contemporary importance to the church. And the whole correspondence throbs with life and love. It is a very attractive part of the New Testament to study.

On the other hand, there are difficulties which, I fancy, keep 1 and 2 Corinthians a closed book to most church members. The word has gone round that they are too difficult: tongues, prophecy and veiled women in 1 Corinthians, coupled with much obscurity in 2 Corinthians about precisely whom Paul is attacking, and why he is getting so worked up about it. So, apart from passages like 1 Corinthians 13 on love, 12 or 14 on spiritual gifts, or 15 on the resurrection, or 2 Corinthians 8 or 9 on giving, the books do not receive the study they deserve from the ordinary church member for whom, after all, they were written.

I want to stimulate people to examine for themselves this remarkable record of the relations between the greatest of church planters and one of the most influential communities he founded and cared for. I want people to see how relevant the problems and the solutions of first-century Corinth are for us today. And in order to highlight this, I propose to select some topics of importance in this correspondence and devote a short chapter to each. Naturally, the chapters will not all be uniform in length, either because of the relative importance of the topics or because of the length of Paul's handling of them in these letters. There will be no attempt at verse by verse exposition and application. Nor shall I try to cover all the major themes in these letters: but simply to show how Paul speaks directly to us over a broad range of issues in the Christian life, and speaks with an incisiveness, clarity and authority that are rare.

But first, let us put these letters in their historical perspective. Corinth was a Roman *colonia*, rebuilt in 46 B.C. after lying waste for a hundred years. Here the proconsul of Achaea had his capital city after 27 B.C. Here Latin was the official tongue.

Corinth was also a Greek port of great importance, situated on the narrow neck of land separating the central part of Greece from the Peloponnesus. As such it had a polyglot community, a plethora of Greek philosophers and many Jews, attracted by commerce.

Corinth was, moreover, an Oriental city in morals and religion. The worship of Aphrodite and Astarte, Isis and Osiris made cult prostitution the order of the day, and gave women, even women priests, such a notorious place that it is easy to see why Paul insisted that it was a shame for a woman to go unveiled and to teach in the Christian assemblies.

It was to this mixed community at Corinth, greedy for power, dedicated to pleasure, fascinated by rhetoric and knowledge, that Paul came and preached the gospel during his so-called Second Missionary Journey in the autumn of A.D. 50. His preaching, ably supported by Aquila and Priscilla, was very successful (Acts 18:1f.), so he stayed at Corinth for eighteen months and more before moving back to Antioch. Meanwhile a man named Apollos was converted, was built up by Aquila and Priscilla (who had now moved to Ephesus), and came to Corinth, where he made a great impression on the church (Acts 18:27). Later on, Paul spent the winter months of A.D. 56–7 in Corinth, during which he wrote the Epistle to the Romans. So much is reasonably certain. All else in his relations with Corinth has to be derived by inference from his letters. That is difficult, and there have been many reconstructions, but we are probably right in envisaging some such outline as this.

During his three-year stay in Ephesus from *c.*A.D.53–6 (Acts 19:8–11) Paul heard of gross immorality at Corinth, and wrote urging them to steer clear of it at all costs. This letter is referred to in 1 Cor. 5:9. Part of it may even survive in 2 Cor. 6:14–7:1, but I think this unlikely.

A little later Paul heard of further trouble, and received a letter from Corinth asking for advice (1 Cor. 7:1). In reply he wrote 1 Corinthians from Ephesus before Pentecost (1 Cor. 16:8–9) c.A.D. 54. He also asked Timothy to go and see them after visiting Northern Greece (Acts 19:22, 1 Cor. 4:17, 16:10). It is clear from these allusions that he was afraid that Timothy, a gentle character, might be snubbed. Was he, perhaps, the 'one who suffered the wrong' (2 Cor. 7:12)? Paul says his own plan was to come later, via the northern land route through Macedonia (1 Cor. 16:5).

However, after sending 1 Corinthians, bad news seems to have suggested a change of plan (2 Cor. 1:15f.). The new idea was to give them the benefit of a double visit: to go to Corinth by sea, then on to Macedonia, then return to Corinth before going to Jerusalem with his 'collection for the saints'. But he changed this plan too (2 Cor. 1:15f.). He visited Corinth personally and at once. It must have been a peculiarly horrible experience because he can only bring himself to allude to it in the most roundabout way (2 Cor. 2:1, 13:1). So painful was this visit that Paul sailed straight back to Ephesus. It would seem that he was violently rebuffed by one faction in the church, though others remained loyal to him (see 2 Cor. 2:5–6), and read between the lines of chapters 10:5–12, 11:12–21, 12:19–21. He retired in chagrin and wrote them a letter, 'out of much affliction and anguish of heart and with many tears' (2 Cor. 2:4). This he sent by the hand of Titus, and immediately regretted (2 Cor. 7:5–8, 12, 13). So anxious was he about its possible effect in destroying the church that he could not contain himself, but went up towards Macedonia hoping to meet Titus on his return: he contacted him in Troas, and was overjoyed by the good news of its reception at Corinth and powerful effect in inducing repentance and renewed loyalty. In his relief and joy he wrote 2 Corinthians (or, maybe, chapters 1–9, for many scholars believe that we have part of his 'severe letter' in 2 Corinthians 10–13). Not long afterwards he made his final visit to the city, and ministered among the congregation there for a winter before his fateful visit to Jerusalem with the collection in the spring of A.D. 57 which led to the riot, his arrest, and the start of his long imprisonments in Caesarea and Rome.

In short, Paul must have visited Corinth on at least three occasions, and he wrote them at least four letters, two of them completely or partially lost.

So much for the background. It highlights the progress – and the problems – of Paul's love affair with this ebullient church he had brought into being. We shall now turn to the main issues he felt obliged to handle; they are still highly controversial in Christian circles.

The Corinthian correspondence contains a bagful of topics, and they are handled in no very obvious order by the apostle. The same might be said of the chapters which follow, but that would not be entirely true! Chapters 2–8 deal with aspects of church life as a whole: church founding, baptism, the eucharist, body life, love, worship and prophecy. Chapters 9–14 deal with concerns of individual Christians or sections of the church: the intellect, freedom, giving, sex, suffering and death. The final three chapters examine the leadership of the church, the place of women and the apostolic authority on which it must all rest. I believe that all these issues are crucial to church life today.

PART ONE

Problems for the Church

CHAPTER TWO

MISSION

Let us begin at the beginning, with mission. It is in many circles an unfashionable concept now: it certainly was then. Yet the Corinthian church was born in mission, and mission remained a top priority both in their minds and that of St Paul. It might be instructive to refresh our minds as to how it all started.

CHURCH PLANTING AT CORINTH

The church at Corinth began through the efforts of one man (Acts 18:1). Paul was totally committed to the good news of Jesus. He had made immense sacrifices for it. He wanted his whole life to count in spreading it. And after a time of very moderate success and sparse encouragement at Athens, he moved across to the capital of Greece, Corinth.

God often seems to stimulate initiatives in this way. Rarely does a commission or a committee found a church. It is much more likely to emerge from one dedicated Christian who cannot keep quiet about his Master. Such a man was Vittorio Landero in Nueva Estaçion in Colombia a few years ago. Once this man found Christ he simply had to tell others. He sold his bar, abolished his brothel, and took to the road to share with passers-by the good news that had changed his life. When missionaries penetrated to his part of the country, they found hundreds of Christians there already, and the name they heard everywhere was Vittorio Landero. St Paul must have been like that: a man with one passion.

But a second feature soon emerges. Paul was no individualist. No sooner did he arrive in Corinth than he set about searching for Christian fellowship. He found it in Aquila and Priscilla, a Jewish couple lately arrived from Italy (Acts 18:2). Although the initiative in evangelism often comes from one individual, it takes root and flourishes when carried out in partnership. A team can *demonstrate* the good news in their mutual relationships, as well as merely *talking* about it.

A third important hint to church planters is this. The partnership with Aquila and Priscilla, which began in the most natural way with shared professional interests and similar background, led on to the three of them sharing a household together (Acts 18:3). This both produced mutual appreciation and trust, and also initiated a cell which was able to withstand the fierce opposition that was soon to come. When Christians actually share their home, it generally becomes a powerful springboard for the growth of the gospel. This was one of the most impressive sides of the Jesus People in the 1960s, and remains an attractive aspect of vital Christianity all over the world.

Fourthly, this partnership led to speaking opportunities (Acts 18:4). Paul was invited to speak in the synagogue. He had to earn that right by waiting and worshipping. But when it came his way, he used it powerfully. Recently I met in America a man who adopted a somewhat similar procedure. He found himself in a Presbyterian church that was not very lively. Instead of criticising, he stayed with them and put his back into his membership of that church. After a couple of years or so they asked him to undertake a teaching role. They found out, also, that he had evangelistic gifts. Soon he had brought into being a remarkable house-church of new converts. And instead of this becoming a breakaway movement, he had so won the confidence and respect of his Presbyterian church that they seconded him to look after that new congregation. His ministry is now not only the most exciting one in town, but it is exercised in close amity with the leadership of the parent church.

Fifth, Paul's message was significant in the establishment of this new congregation. He tells us in 1 Cor. 1:18 that it was the message of the cross which he proclaimed continuously, and almost to the exclusion of all else (1 Cor. 2:2). This appeared folly to 'those who are perishing', but 'those who are being saved' found it the power of God. What could be more ludicrous than to maintain in sophisticated Greek circles that God's wisdom and salvation lay in a despised and executed criminal? What could be more blasphemous to Jewish hearers than the suggestion that God's promised deliverance lay in a crucified man exposed in shame on his cross? Yet those who believed found that cross to be both the wisdom and the power of God: God's wisdom in humbling pride and rescuing the hopeless, and God's power in breaking through the barriers of guilt and alienation which kept Jews and Greeks alike from God.

But it seems that Paul only became thrilled, or 'gripped' with the message, as the original of Acts 18:5 puts it, when Silas and Timothy came and joined him. No doubt their shared times of studying the scriptures and of preaching in the streets encouraged one another very much. We all need encouragement, and Paul certainly did. So much so that God spoke to him in a vision one night, 'Do not be afraid, but speak and do not be silent; for I am with you and no man shall attack you to harm you; for I have many people in this city' (Acts 18:10). Evangelism is a draining task, and greatly needs the encouragement of brother Christians and the Lord himself. If a man is too brash to need encouragement, then he is too insensitive to be much good as an evangelist.

A sixth factor which is significant at Corinth is the cultural spread of the converts. They seem to have come from every background in the city. There was Titius Justus, a distinguished Gentile, sympathetic to Judaism; Crispus, the ruler of the synagogue (that certainly created a stir!); and such men as Erastus the city treasurer, and Quartus, whose name suggests he was a Roman citizen. But Paul was also concerned to reach the rough element in town, and men and women came to Christ from the steaming alleys of this seaport: the prostitutes and the thieves, the homosexuals and the idolaters, the drunks and the nobodies (1 Cor. 6:9–11). The gospel spread among every stratum of the population. It still does when it is proclaimed and lived with imagination, faith and courage.

Seventh, Paul took trouble over the converts. He was no fly-by-night evangelist who was always moving on somewhere else. To be sure, he did not stay long in some of the places he visited. His length of stay seems generally to have been determined by the strategic importance of the place and the measure of response. But always he seems to have taken care to provide for the growth of the new believers. One of the weaknesses of much modern evangelism is that there is plenty of challenging for a verdict, but very little building up. Paul stayed with these new Christians for 'a year and six months, teaching the word of God among them' (Acts 18:11). Often nowadays there is no such care, no such agony of soul over new converts, as is portrayed in Paul's Corinthian correspondence. His evangelism had a solid teaching base. So ought ours to have. A church where there are many conversions each year needs to have regular Beginners' Groups into which new believers are put. And then, when they have grown in the Lord, they can be transferred to one of the house groups which belong to the local church. Thus results are conserved, and believers grow.

Those seven principles which Paul used in his church planting might with profit be applied by Christians in many parts of the world.

CHURCH LIFE IN MISSION

If the Christian church at Corinth was to emulate some of the evangelistic zeal that had brought their community into being, what qualities would the apostle expect to see in them?

Time and again in these letters Paul writes to the Corinthians as 'brothers'. This was no mere polite form of address. These men and women had actually come into an intimate brother and sister relationship through their incorporation in the family of God. The quality of their mutual love, respect and care must mark them out if they are to have any impact on surrounding paganism.

Furthermore, they must realise that they will always be in a minority, and often an uninfluential and despised minority at that (1 Cor. 1:26–31). They may not number many noble or wise members, by worldly standards. They will be no more than yeast in the dough of society (1 Cor. 5:7). But this must not dismay them, or give them a chip on the shoulder. Their Master was constantly in a minority, and it did not bother him, because he knew he was in the right.

It perhaps goes without saying that these were very exciting and interesting people to meet. There was nothing dull, narrow or monochrome about them. The fact that they had become Christians certainly had not made grey men of them, as every line of these letters indicate most forcibly. That is not always the case with modern Christians.

They had their faults, and these are not glossed over by Paul. But they made you feel at home, and laid themselves out for you (1 Cor. 16:15). Their homes spelt 'welcome' and that was extremely attractive. Evangelism is not possible in a community unless the homes of the people are warm and welcoming.

Whatever excesses you detected in their worship services from time to time, it could not be denied that in their assembly you sensed the reality of God (1 Cor. 14:24f.). Unless that is present in a congregation of Christian people, no amount of talking about the faith will do any good.

Paul sometimes expresses his hopes for the church in very evocative imagery. Here are four of the examples he used. There are others.

He saw the Corinthians as an open letter, to be read by all and sundry (2 Cor. 3:2). The greatest recommendation any preacher can have is the lives of those who have come to faith in Christ through him. Paul sees their lives as an open letter, written by Christ not with ink but with the Holy Spirit. When Christian characters are open to inspection like that, and reveal the work of Christ in them, then others are readily attracted.

Again, Paul saw the Christians as an attractive smell! He must have had a sense of humour to express himself thus. 'We are the aroma of Christ,' he writes (2 Cor. 2:15). And like any aroma, this one either attracts or repels. In the part of town where I live, Don Miller's Hot Bread Kitchen has recently been installed. It has a roaring custom. Why? Not only because its products are good and wholesome, but because you can smell it a couple of streets away! When Christians are right with their Lord, a similar attractive aroma emanates from their lives.

As we shall see later on, the apostle is very impressed with the image of the Body of Christ (1 Corinthians 12). If Christ is indeed 'embodied' in the people, then their mutual relationships are the strongest attraction to draw separated limbs into the Body. It is only through the Body that Christ can make himself known in any place. To that extent he depends on his people.

Perhaps the most famous image of the outward look of the church in these letters is that of the embassy (2 Cor. 5:20). The ambassador represents his king and country in a foreign land. The courtesy, the consistency, the clarity and persuasiveness of the ambassador are all necessary qualities in a church if it is going to make favourable impact for Jesus Christ. 'So we are ambassadors for Christ, God making his appeal through us. We beseech you on behalf of Christ, be reconciled to God.'

22

CHURCH LEADERS IN MISSION

Paul realised that Christian leaders in general, and apostles in particular, have a special responsibility in the area of mission. He wrestles with it in chapters 3–6 of 2 Corinthians. Perhaps chapter 4 brings us to the heart of what he has to say. How is it that this amazing man Paul seems so tireless in his evangelism? Why does he never give up?

1. Paul handles the *endurance* of the Christian minister at the very outset of the chapter. He is flesh and blood like the rest of us. He is tempted to play the coward, to lose heart (2 Cor. 4:1, 16). What keeps him going? He suggests three reasons.

First, he had been given this ministry: he was entrusted with it by God. That God should have chosen *him* was a constant source of amazement. He had been a blasphemer, less than the least of all Christians, the chief of sinners (Eph. 3:8, 1 Tim. 1:12f.)! Why should God bother with him? He saw his ministry as an amazing privilege.

Second, he saw himself as deeply in debt to the Lord. 'By the mercy of God,' he wrote (2 Cor. 4:1). He could not earn it. Sheer, unmerited grace had found him, rebel that he was, on the Damascus road, and made a new man of him. In the light of that mercy, he could not contemplate giving up.

And the third factor in his endurance was the constant inner strength supplied by the Holy Spirit. He begins the chapter with a conscious reference back to the words at the end of chapter 3. 'Therefore,' he says, 'we do not lose heart.' Why not? Because of the liberation and the growing Christlikeness which the Spirit of God produces in the believer. That is why he cannot give up.

2. The minister's endurance in this whole work of mission is matched by his *resolve*. It appears in 2 Cor. 4:2. If he is to fulfil his ministry both to the congregation and to those who watch critically from the wings, he must have nothing to do with disgraceful, underhand ways. His life and his message must be open and clear. He must allow no compromise of intellect or heart. Paul was accused by his

detractors of acting from self-interest and diluting the gospel. But he was neither unscrupulous politician nor ingratiating salesman. His life was open to inspection at every point.

3. The minister's *concern* is next brought before us (2 Cor. 4:3–4). Paul realises that the spread of Christianity is no intellectual game. It is a spiritual battle. There is a very real foe, 'the god of this world', opposing Christ every step of the way. Paul is clear that people are 'perishing' without his gospel, and here he echoes the uncompromising teaching of the whole of the New Testament. Men are either being saved or lost, they are either wheat or tares, either on the broad way or the narrow, either in Christ or not. There is no middle ground. Paul recalls that his own commission from the Lord is 'to open their eyes, that they may turn from darkness to light, and from the power of Satan to God' (Acts 26:18). But Satan is active to prevent this. Like Jesus before him, Paul does not waste time arguing the existence of Satan. He knows from experience the reality of this malign anti-God force, the great outside hindrance to the spread of the gospel. He calls him 'the god of this world', and a very apt name it is. Jesus had called him the same. Behind the materialism and apathy of our society there is an evil, intelligent, hostile power. Satan has one overmastering purpose. It is 'to keep them from seeing the light of the gospel of the glory of Christ, who is the likeness of God'. He does not mind how civilised or moral people are, if only he can keep them from Christ. And to this end he has a deadly weapon, blindness. 'The god of this world has blinded the minds . . .' He persuades them that the gospel is false, or dull, or narrowing, or unnecessary. If ever a man is to have any effect in evangelising people, he needs to come to terms with this unwelcome reality of the satanic force, utterly opposed to the gospel, hindering its spread at every turn. He has to realise that without Christ people are perishing. Otherwise there will be no motivation sufficient to mobilise him and counteract his natural lethargy. Only when we see that people are perishing without

the gospel by which we live, will we bestir ourselves to help them. But how?

4. So Paul goes on to consider the *methods* of the Christian minister in evangelism. They are interesting. First, the consistent life mentioned in 2 Cor. 4:2 is obviously indispensable. Then there is the deep love indicated in verse 15, 'it is all for your sake'; or verse 5 'what we preach is not ourselves . . . ourselves your servants for Jesus' sake'. That readiness to serve others to the utmost, that willingness for death to be at work in us provided it means life in others (2 Cor. 4:12) is an essential element in evangelism. People will see from our earnestness that this is a vital matter of spiritual life and death, and that we are willing to put our own lives on the line for them. Then they will listen. I think we can assume here what Paul states so clearly elsewhere (e.g. Eph. 6:18–20) that prayer is one of the most important ways in which people are brought to faith. How else can we cooperate with the God who shines into the heart against the god who blinds the mind (2 Cor. 4:4, 6)? If prayer is beamed on a person, it is a marvellous way of softening up that heart for the gospel. 'You also burrow underneath by prayer for us,' writes Paul in the Greek of 2 Cor. 1:11. The thought is of undermining the redoubts of a castle by tunnelling. That is what the unseen but powerful ministry of prayer does. It undermines resistance to the gospel. Then the way is clear for fearless preaching. 'We preach . . . Jesus Christ as Lord' (2 Cor. 4:5). Christ, the climax of all history: Jesus, the Saviour; Lord, the master of their lives. No dilettante preaching here, no shallow Jesus, no cheap grace.

5. This leads Paul on to draw the veil aside for a moment on the minister's *sacrifice*. The minister has to be willing to be their servant for Jesus' sake. Not their boss, their priest, their leader; but their slave, continuing and embodying the servanthood of Jesus. He has to be delivered up to death for Jesus' sake, so that the life of Jesus can flow without hindrance through his mortal body. (2 Cor. 4:11). Externally this will mean vulnerability to mockery, hardship,

illness and physical death. Inwardly it will mean that the proud self must daily be put where it belongs, on the cross of our lives, so that the indwelling Christ may have his proper place on the throne. Without that self-sacrifice, that 'treasure in earthen vessels', men will not perceive that 'the transcendent power belongs to God and not to us' (2 Cor. 4:7).

6. But there is a wonderful *reward* for this sort of sacrificial evangelism. It is twofold. There is the reward of seeing others respond to Christ. And there is no joy like that. 'Though you have countless guides in Christ, you do not have many fathers. For I became your father in Christ Jesus through the gospel,' he says (1 Cor. 4:15). The Corinthians themselves were his reward.

But there is a more personal and interior reward awaiting the faithful Christian worker; the enjoyment of heaven for ever with the Lord. There is nothing wrong with looking forward to this. Paul did, and it is an aspect of Christianity that has dropped out very much these days, to our loss. 'We do not lose heart,' he writes. 'Though our outer nature is wasting away; our inner nature is being renewed every day. For this slight momentary affliction is preparing for us an eternal weight of glory beyond all comparison' (2 Cor. 4:16–17). Heaven is our home. Like the village blacksmith, we have our workshop below, but our residence above.

CHURCH ATTITUDES IN MISSION

With such a community and such ministers, what are the proper attitudes in reaching out with the gospel? What should we rely on?

Paul was a travelling evangelist. They should not neglect such a man. He had great gifts in evangelism. But equally they should not unduly rely on men like him. A visitor could only add impetus to the mission in which they were already engaged within their community. If they were not already involved, he could not do their task for them. The same holds good today.

There is a lovely little cameo on the proper approach to

mission, for local church and visiting evangelist alike, in 1 Cor. 2:1–5.

In this passage Paul tells how he approached his mission in Corinth when he first came and preached the gospel to them. It is highly significant. Able though he was, experienced though he was, he came in weakness and in dependence on God alone. 'I was with you in weakness and in much fear and trembling' (1 Cor. 2:3). He came in 'fear', a trembling anxiety to do the job well. He came with great simplicity: 'My speech and my message were not in plausible words of wisdom.' There was no reliance on ability (*sophia*) or oratory (*logos*), both highly prized at Corinth. His reliance was on the cross of Jesus, and this he proclaimed (1 Cor. 2:2). He was bold to preach the cross, however weak and foolish it seemed. He knew it to be the power of God (1 Cor. 1:18).

As this uncompromising and unfashionable message was preached, Paul knew men and women would be challenged to respond. They could either believe it or reject it. Paul was not interested in intellectual or emotional conquest. He was after the *faith* of his hearers 'that your faith might not rest in the wisdom of men but in the power of God' (1 Cor. 2:5). Faith does not save anyone. It is Christ who saves, but faith puts a man in touch with him. That is why it is criminal for a preacher to draw attention to himself, by the brilliance of his content or his eloquence. He is nothing but a signpost to Christ.

And when someone puts his faith in Christ he begins to discover the 'demonstration of the Spirit and of power' (1 Cor. 2:4). It is nothing to do with emotionalism, though emotions may well be stirred. It is nothing to do with human appeal, though a preacher may well be the agent. No, God's Spirit, God's power, comes into every heart, however weak, which entrusts itself to Christ.

This attitude of humble trust in the Saviour, the message, and the Spirit characterised both church and evangelist when they were at their best. No doubt they had their off days.

MISSION PREACHING

It might be well to conclude this chapter with a closer look at the message in evangelism as indicated in these two letters to Corinth. There would seem to have been at least four major elements, not always found in modern proclamation of the gospel.

1. The main burden of Paul's message was the grace of God, the sheer, undreamed-of mercy of God to sinful human beings. 'Working together with him', he cries, 'we entreat you not to accept the grace of God in vain' (2 Cor. 6:1). He shares this message with an attractive warmth, but does not disguise what it cost him. 'We are treated as impostors, and yet are true; as unknown, and yet well known; as dying, and behold we live; as punished, and yet not killed; as sorrowful, yet always rejoicing; as poor, yet making many rich; as having nothing, and yet possessing everything (2 Cor. 6:8–10).

2. He found this message of the boundless grace of God everywhere in the scriptures of the Old Testament. He preached constantly out of those scriptures, focusing attention on Christ and preaching in the power of his Spirit. He was a profound believer in the unity of revelation, as even a cursory glance at chapter 3 of 2 Corinthians will make plain. He would not dream of setting the God of the Old Testament against the God of the New. He saw Christ as the fulfilment of the law and the prophets. He perceived foreshadowings of the Saviour in even the most obscure corners of the Old Testament, and he was not afraid to argue with the Jews out of their own scriptures.

3. Supremely, he saw the cross of Christ in those scriptures. And the cross was the third and most characteristic element in Paul's proclamation of the gospel. He understood it in a variety of modes.

The cross is folly to the unconverted mind (1 Cor. 1:18f.). Paul was well aware that it is folly to tell the Greek that ultimate wisdom resides in a particular, or to tell the Jew that his Messiah has come, all unrecognised, and has ended up under the curse of God upon the cross – for 'a hanged man is accursed by God' (Deut. 21:23). Yes, Paul knew it would seem folly, but he persisted in proclaiming it to all and sundry. Why?

Because the cross meant sinbearing. Nowhere does Paul make this more clear than in his staggering words in 2 Cor. 5:21, 'For our sake he made him [Jesus] to be sin who knew no sin, so that in him we might become the righteousness of God.' Jesus became what we are, in order that we might become what he is. Christ entered into our humanity and doom on the cross so that he might be able to offer believers the seamless robe of his perfection. No wonder the second century author of the *Epistle to Diognetus* (chapter 9) bursts out, 'What else could cover our sins but his righteousness? In whom else was it possible that we, the wicked and ungodly, could be justified except in the Son of God alone? O sweet exchange, O work of God beyond all searching out! O benefits surpassing all expectations! That the wickedness of the many should be hid in a single righteous one, and that the righteousness of One should justify many transgressors!'

Another aspect of the cross, which makes considerable appeal in today's troubled industrial and social scene, is that of reconciliation (2 Cor. 5:18f.). Paul does not use the word in quite the same way as we do. For on the one hand he says, 'God, who through Christ has reconciled us to himself' and on the other, 'we beseech you on behalf of Christ, be reconciled to God'. That would be nonsense in normal English usage. There would be no point in urging those who are already reconciled to become reconciled! But the Greek word really means 'remove the barriers to fellowship', and that makes admirable sense. For a double wall of partition separates us from God. On the one hand, there is the wall of our rebellion and sin; on the other, there is the wall of God's rightful judgment against our wickedness. On the cross God broke down the wall of his judgment which kept us insulated from him. He did it through allowing that wall to fall on himself, as in Christ he took its full weight, for 'in Christ, God was reconciling the world to himself' (2 Cor. 5:19). Our wall remains, and that is why Paul beseeches men to be reconciled to God. They must pull down the wall of their rebellion and come back to God in sincere repentance. Then there will be no barrier to fellowship. Both walls lie in ruins. Reconciliation is complete. What a magnificent explanation of the cross!

Paul has a third picture of the cross. It is like a magnet. It draws men to the Saviour. 'For the love of Christ controls us,' wrote the apostle, 'because we are convinced that one has died for all' (2 Cor. 5:14). The cross is the supreme drawing power of God for sinners. He shows us by that cross that our guilt has failed to alienate him. He loves us still, although we have sided with the very people who nailed him there. 'I, if I be lifted up from the earth will draw all men to me,' he had once predicted. It came true. The cross is the supreme magnet.

And therefore Paul sees the cross, folly though speaking of it be, as fundamental to the Christian proclamation. 'I delivered to you as of first importance what I also received, that Christ died for our sins in accordance with the scriptures,' he wrote (1 Cor. 15:3). The cross is the centrepiece of the gospel. It takes us to the heart of God who cares, is involved, takes responsibility, and goes on loving though our sins torture him. It is the most wonderful thing in the world. Horrible gallows though it be, it has been transfigured by the self-offering of Jesus the Messiah. Because of that cross there is good news to proclaim, and Paul for one was not going to be backward in telling it.

4. The grace of God, taught in the scriptures and most clearly demonstrated in the cross of Christ, challenges men to respond. 'If Jesus Christ be God and died for me, no sacrifice can be too great for me to make for him,' said C. T. Studd, the England cricketer at the end of the last century who became a missionary on three continents. His logic is unassailable. And therefore Paul pressed the claims of Christ on people throughout the Mediterranean basin. He challenged them to respond, and he used two spurs in that direction. One was warning, and the other appeal.

Warning is very unfashionable these days. The thought that sin might be punished or alienation from God finalised is too awful to contemplate. We relegate hell fire preaching to the wicked Victorians or the lunatic hot-gospelling fringe. But Paul was certainly not afraid to mention the consequences of rejecting God's way of salvation. 'We must all appear before the judgment seat of Christ', he reminded them (2 Cor. 5:10). 'Do you not realise that Jesus Christ is in you? – unless indeed you fail to meet the test!' (2 Cor. 13:5).

Equally, he was not afraid to appeal to his hearers. Most preachers fail to be effective in evangelism because they have never learned to plead with men. Not so Paul. 'Our mouth is open to you, Corinthians; our heart is wide. Open your hearts to us' (2 Cor. 6:11, 7:2). 'Behold, now is the accepted time; behold, now is the day of salvation' (2 Cor. 6:2). 'We beseech you on behalf of Christ, be reconciled to God' (2 Cor. 5:20). So long as a man is confronted fairly and squarely by what Christ has done, I can see no reason why an evangelist should not urge response because of the consequences in the future, and because of gratitude to the Saviour. Yet warning and appeal must be used sparingly and judiciously. The hymn puts it well:

> My God, I love thee, not because
> I hope for heaven thereby,
> Nor yet because who love thee not
> Are lost eternally.
>
> Thou, O my Jesus, thou didst me
> Upon the cross embrace;
> For me didst bear the nails and spear,
> And manifold disgrace,
>
> And griefs and torments numberless
> And sweat of agony;
> Yea, death itself – and all for me
> Who was thine enemy.

Then why, O blessed Jesus Christ,
Should I not love thee well?
Not for the sake of gaining heaven
Nor of escaping hell;

Not for the hope of gaining aught,
Nor seeking a reward;
But as thyself hast loved me
O ever-loving Lord.

Paul would have approved of that hymn. It underlines his approach to mission.

CHAPTER THREE

BAPTISM

If mission is a controversial subject, so is baptism. It arouses strong passions among Christians. On the whole Catholics maintain that baptism is what makes a man a Christian, and that it should therefore be administered widely and as early as possible in life. Most Protestants see baptism as the seal on repentance and faith, and hold that it should preferably be administered after profession of faith in Christ. And Pentecostals tend to give the impression that the only baptism which really matters is baptism in the Holy Spirit, the mark of which is the ability to speak in tongues. What has Paul to say to all this?

WHAT DOES BAPTISM MEAN?
Baptism is a big word, as big as the salvation of which it is the sacrament. Paul does not give sustained teaching on the subject in these letters, but he does make four points of substance about it. In a little-known part of 1 Corinthians (10:2f.), he compares Jesus to Moses, and Christian baptism to the Israelites' passage through the Red Sea under Moses' leadership.

First, baptism means *commitment*. Just as the Israelites were committed to Moses through their crossing of the Red Sea, so Christians are committed to Christ through their baptism. It is no magic charm, has no social function: it signifies nothing less than lifelong commitment to Jesus. And naturally, if it is administered to children, its meaning must be made plain to them and its challenge roundly put to them when they are old enough to respond. Baptism is the pledge of commitment: in the imagery of 1 Peter 3:21 (Greek) it is the oath of allegiance of a soldier joining up.

Second, baptism means *incorporation*. Paul uses a very strange phrase in 1 Corinthians 10:2, which shows how the practice of Christian baptism has affected the Moses illustration. He says that the Israelites were 'baptized *into* Moses in the cloud and in the sea'. This is obviously coloured by the Christian use of 'baptize into Christ' which is logically and grammatically very strange, but none the less very important. The New Testament's favourite description of a Christian is someone who is 'in Christ'. But it is equally insistent that nobody arrives there by accident, by birth, by religious observance or by doing lots of good things. We are by nature 'having no hope and without God in the world' (Eph. 2:12). But God has acted for us in the coming, the death and the resurrection of Jesus. Our sins can be forgiven because he has taken responsibility for them. We are 'in Adam' by birth, part of the old fallen humanity headed up by the first man. We can be 'in Christ' by the new birth, part of the new humanity headed up by the Last Man. Baptism is the sacrament of incorporation. It is the bridge by which we pass from being *without* Christ to being *in* Christ. You cannot live and rest in Christ until you have come into Christ. Baptism is the sacrament of that journey.

Third, baptism means *death and resurrection*. Figuratively, that is what happened to the Israelites as they went through the walls of water on either side of them in the Red Sea. It was a death to all that lay in Egypt. It meant a complete break with the past, its doom and its bondage. It opened new vistas of hope for a Promised Land. It was no less than a death to the old life and a door into the new. That is what baptism means, and many Jewish and Muslim

34

people understand that very well. When one of their children becomes baptised they tend to hold a funeral for him. They see him as dead. That is a point which Romans 6 brings out very clearly. In baptism we die to the old life, and rise with Christ to all that the future holds with him. Manifestly, therefore, baptism is the microcosm of the whole Christian life.

Fourth, baptism means *justification*. It is made clear in 1 Cor. 6:11 that the drunkards, homosexuals, thieves and others who formed the Corinthian church had been washed (in baptism) and had been justified in the name of the Lord Jesus and in the Spirit of our God. Sometimes Protestants have set justification over against baptism. 'I was christened as a kid, but now I want to get properly baptised because I've been converted', is the sort of thing one sometimes hears, but it would have sounded very strange to New Testament ears. For it divides what God has united. Baptism is the sacrament of justification by God's grace. Justification is for the totally unqualified: so is baptism. Justification leads to a life of holiness: so does baptism. Justification is once and for all and unrepeatable: so is baptism. Justification is done for us, and we cannot contribute to it one whit: the same is true of baptism. They stand or fall together. Both point to the amazing initiative of God for sinners. Both point to man's need to respond to that initiative in faith and surrender. They are the outside and the inside of the same thing. Therefore baptism should never be denigrated, as if it were unimportant. It should never be lionised, as if it stood irrespective of repentance and faith. And it should never be repeated: that is as illogical as to be rejustified!

IS BAPTISM IN THE HOLY SPIRIT SOMETHING DIFFERENT FROM WATER BAPTISM?
We are heading for trouble when we start using interpretative glosses for Bible phrases. The Bible does not speak of 'water baptism' and 'Spirit baptism' as many moderns do. We would be wise to stick to Bible language if we are not

further to confuse a complicated situation. I am aware of only one place in the New Testament where the distinction could be made (since the 'Ephesian dozen' in Acts 19 were not Christians at all). That is the case of the Samaritans in Acts 8. They were baptised, but we are told that the Spirit had not yet fallen upon them. The reason, I believe, was because the age-old split between Jews and Samaritans had not been healed. Had the Spirit been given before the Jewish-Christian leaders came down from Jerusalem and laid hands upon them in reconciliation and solidarity, there would have been two distinct denominations at the very outset of Christianity, utterly out of communion with one another.

That passage apart, the New Testament does not distinguish between water baptism and baptism 'in' or 'with' (the same Greek word is used for both, so any attempt to build a theology on the difference is ludicrous!) the Holy Spirit. There are seven references to baptism in the Holy Spirit, six of them referring to the contrast between John the Baptist who baptised in water, and Jesus who would baptise in the Holy Spirit. Mark 1:8, Matt. 3:11, Luke 3:16 and John 1:33 look forward to this baptism in the Spirit, as does Acts 1:5. At Pentecost it happened, and Acts 11:16 looks back to it. So much for six of the references. They are quite unambiguous, and refer to the contrast between the days of preparation when John preached repentance, and the days of the Spirit which Jesus would inaugurate. The only other reference to baptism in the Holy Spirit comes in 1 Cor. 12:13, where it is made abundantly plain that not just the tongues speakers, not just the miracle workers, but *all* the Corinthian Christians had been baptised in the Holy Spirit and had drunk of his waters. Just as we are not to separate baptism from justification, so we are not to separate it from the gift of the Holy Spirit. 'Any one who does not have the Spirit of Christ does not belong to him' (Rom. 8:9).

Naturally, this does not mean that the coming of the Spirit must be contemporaneous with our baptism or our awareness of justification. Quite often all three happen at different times. A person may be baptised as a child, believe as a teenager and be set free to enjoy his inheritance of the Spirit years later. But the point is that they belong together. From the point of view of the church, baptism is what makes a man a Christian. From the point of view of the individual, his own repentance and faith are the important thing. From God's point of view, what matters is his receiving the Holy Spirit who makes him a member of God's family. But they are three strands in a single rope which binds a Christian to his Lord.

It is obviously possible (and widespread) for those who have been baptised to show no sign whatever of the new birth: 'He is not a real Jew who is one outwardly,' wrote Paul about entry into the old covenant, 'nor is true circumcision something external and physical. He is a Jew who is one inwardly, and real circumcision is a matter of the heart, spiritual and not literal' (Rom. 2:28–9). External formalities alone never saved anyone, and baptism will not if devoid of repentance, faith and the gift of God's Holy Spirit. But nevertheless the three belong together in the purposes of God. They jointly form the way of Christian initiation. And a man is not a Christian until he has all three: baptism, repentance and faith issuing in justification, and the gift of the Spirit. Later in his Christian life he may well receive the gift of tongues, or some other mark of the Spirit's presence. Fine. But let him not call it baptism. The New Testament does not, and he will only spread confusion if he does!

WHO SHOULD ADMINISTER BAPTISM?

Paul does not tell us. It might naturally fall to the acknowledged Christian leader in the community, which is why Paul tries to rack his brains to remember whom he had baptised personally. But actually it does not appear to matter. Baptism is a symbolic action to make real what God does for a man: its efficacy is not dependent upon the right administrant. As a matter of interest, Paul seems rarely to have baptised people. He saw his role as an evangelist and a church builder, not as someone who regularly administered the sacrament of baptism, though on occasion he would do so (1 Cor. 1:13–17). It is interesting that Paul nowhere makes any split between what a 'clergyman' and a 'layman' may do. The very idea is a gross anachronism. Just as it is possible for anyone to baptise in the name of the Lord, it is apparently possible for any Corinthian leader to celebrate the Lord's Supper. When he has to deal with eucharistic abuses at Corinth, he rebukes the whole Corinthian church, not any particular minister. Liturgical functions such as baptism and presiding at the eucharist were not at that time restricted to any particular group of Christians. Perhaps they should not be today, so long as the administrant in either case is a respected and godly member of the congregation. There is no suggestion anywhere in the New Testament that baptism and the celebration of the Communion are tasks reserved for a priestly cadre.

WHO SHOULD RECEIVE BAPTISM?
Believers, without question, should be baptised (1 Cor. 6:11, 12:13). The individuals whom Paul mentions in 1 Cor. 1:14 were first-generation adult believers: Crispus had been head of the synagogue (Acts 18:8) and Gaius acted as host to the church there (Rom. 16:23).

Households also were baptised by Paul. He mentions the household of Stephanas (1 Cor. 1:16). In Acts 16:33 we find Paul baptising the whole family when the Philippian gaoler comes to faith. This sort of thing has caused some embarrassment to Baptists and to paedobaptists alike: the former because the rite was administered to those who are not said to have expressed faith; and the latter because there is no evidence that the baptised families themselves became believers.

But, seen against the background of the ancient world, where the father as head of the family was practically omnipotent, it would have been very surprising if the household (which included slaves and children) were not baptised along with their head. As a Jew Paul would have had the precedent of Old Testament circumcision. The children of believers shared in the sign and seal of the covenant, circumcision, long before they were old enough to understand its implications. Indeed, 'every male throughout your generations, whether born in your house, or bought with your money from any foreigner who is not of your offspring . . . shall be circumcised . . . Any uncircumcised male . . . shall be cut off from his people; he has broken my covenant' (Gen. 17:12–14). There was ample precedent, then, for the baptism of households, and many Christians believe that this still holds good, and that baptism may fittingly be administered to the children of those who are themselves believers, not in order to make the child belong to God but because the child *does* belong to God. He entrusted it to those parents. He died for it and rose again in Christ; and he offers it the pledge of justification and incorporation into his family long before the child itself is able to make any response one way or the other. The initiative has been taken by God. Baptism of households is the sign of the prevenient grace of God who longs to save. In due course it needs to be complemented by the repentance and faith of the youngster, thus making his own what has been made over to him in the intention of God, the donor.

There is one strange passage which has given rise to endless discussion, 1 Cor. 15:39, where Paul alludes to the practice of baptism for the dead. The Mormons have made great play with this. Can one imagine Paul justifying the practice of retrospective baptism, viewed almost magically, as a passport to heaven for members of previous generations? Probably not. You can actually remove the whole problem by re-punctuation! 'What of those who are baptized? For the dead, if the dead are not raised at all. And what is the point of that?' But that savours of special pleading! Probably Paul is citing, without advocating, a practice which had crept in at Corinth: vicarious baptism. Barrett believes it may mean that some people were baptised on behalf of their dead relations who had emphatically been Christians but who had omitted to have themselves baptised while alive. Raeder believes that some people at Corinth underwent Christian baptism in the hope of gaining reunion after death with their departed (Christian) relatives. In any case it is an *ad hominem* argument, designed to point out to the Corinthians the inconsistency of their practice if the dead do not rise.

DOES BAPTISM GIVE ETERNAL SECURITY?

The clear implication of chapter 10 is that it does not. The Corinthians clearly thought it did. Their view of it was, as we have seen, almost magical: the elixir of life, like initiation into the Eleusinian mysteries. Once baptised you could do whatever you liked without imperilling your eternal security with Christ. Hence the catalogue of vices which we meet in 1 Corinthians. They are compatible only with an antinomianism which is secure in the assumption that the baptised will inevitably be saved, whatever they do. Paul warns that this is not so. And he draws the closest parallel he can from the Old Testament.

The Old Testament people had, like the Corinthians, gone through the 'baptismal' waters of the Red Sea. They had been fed by the spiritual food of manna in the desert, which corresponds to Christ feeding the Corinthians with the bread of his body in the eucharist. But all the same they perished. They gave way to immorality and idolatry, to testing the Lord and to grumbling, and they 'were overthrown in the wilderness' (1 Cor. 10:5). 'Now these things happened to them as a warning, but they were written down for our instruction,' says Paul to his careless charges at Corinth. 'Therefore let any one who thinks that he stands take heed lest he fall' (1 Cor. 10:11–12).

Paul could not put it more plainly. To have received baptism and the eucharist is no more guarantee of eternal security for the Corinthian Christians than crossing the Red Sea and eating the manna was for the Israelites. It is those who begin *and continue* with Christ who can be assured of his eternal home. God remains utterly faithful, and yet apostasy remains an awesome possibility. It takes two to make and maintain a relationship. Thus none need despair: if you fear you have committed the unforgivable sin then you cannot possibly have done so. None need despair, but equally, none dare presume. And to sin away one's life while claiming to have been saved, be it by baptism or some profession of conversion long ago, is sheer presumption.

CHAPTER FOUR

THE LORD'S SUPPER

Come, in imagination, to the house of Aquila and Priscilla in Corinth. Aquila is a Christian businessman from North Turkey, Priscilla an upper-crust Roman from the capital. Her family weren't too happy about the marriage, but it is working well, and both are keen Christians. Wherever they go in their far-flung tentmaking business and leather trade their home hosts a Christian church.

Their house in Corinth is, accordingly, quite spacious. It has a portico, a central open room partly roofed and partly open to the fresh air, with a goldfish pond in the centre and a small fountain playing. A number of side rooms open up from the central enclosure where people can pile in, with the main room as the focus.

At around five p.m. people start turning up. Some come from the market, some from the baths. They come for worship, for enjoyment and to spend the evening together in Christian company. They bring and share their food and drink. Ideally there is enough to go round. Then the news is shared, and the instruments are brought out – primitive versions of the flute, violin and guitar. Then one person will suggest a song, a simple one, and they all learn to sing it. We have a number of these songs in the New Testament. There is one in Ephesians, 'Awake, O sleeper, and arise from the dead, and Christ shall give you light.' They sing it, together first, and then as a round. And one or two tell how they did awake from the dead and how Christ's light did break in upon them. They sing a bit more: perhaps some of the ancient psalms of David. There would be a time of teaching from the Old Testament, and the leader would show how those ancient scriptures had been wonderfully fulfilled in Jesus and the lives of the Christians themselves. Perhaps a visiting Christian from Judea would pull out of his pocket a battered list of some of the sayings of Jesus, and these would be learned by heart so as to be applied to their daily lives. Quite likely someone would then stand up in the name of Jesus and give a direct prophetic message to the assembled company, or maybe a message in tongues, with another person to interpret it. One person in a corner would say, 'I've had a mental picture during our time of prayer, and I believe I should share it with you all.' Thus the congregation is thrilled and edified. Then the leader for the evening would say, 'We mustn't go away without recalling what Jesus did to make us his people. He called us out of darkness into his marvellous light, and set us free from the grip of those evil habits that held us in bondage. Let us, then, do as he did – take and eat bread, in remembrance of him. Let us exult in his living presence in our midst tonight. And let us go out tomorrow to serve him with renewed dedication.' They reverently pass the bread from hand to hand, reflecting on what it cost him to allow his body to be broken for them. Then the cup goes round the central room and the side rooms, packed with eager, reverent people. There is silence, then a blessing is said, and quietly they move out into the night and go home prepared to live for their Lord the next day.

That is what it must have been like in the old days: no books, no fixed liturgy, no special building, no monopoly by the clergy, and no sharp distinction between the supper party and the supper of the Lord. It seems to me that there is much here for us to recover.

THEIR STRENGTHS AT CORINTH

The strengths of this type of gathering are considerable.

In the first place, there is a great deal to be said for the eucharist taking place in the home. This makes for intimacy, for naturalness, for sharing. It has obvious dangers, notably sectarianism, but these can be avoided easily enough, provided the leaders of the house group are in regular touch with the leadership of the church at large. Where the church of God in this century has moved over to home Communions in order to complement the larger gatherings in church, it has made for strength.

Second, home Communions facilitated maximum contribution from members. Some of the most memorable Communions I have ever attended have been when people gathered in the home and prayed as they felt led, made contributions of thoughts or scriptural verses that had helped them, offered a prophetic word, surrounded some sick member with prayer and the imposition of hands, and administered the elements to one another.

Third, these Corinthians made no rigid separation between the secular and the sacred. Their love-feast or *agape* was an integral part of the whole evening, part of the context of their self-realisation as the Body of Christ. To be sure, it could be abused, and it was, as we can see from 2 Peter and Jude, with the result that it was discontinued in the second and third centuries. But it is a lovely thing when it is right. To have a love-feast followed by a Communion is a deeply moving experience, and one to which many more Christians should be exposed. It is a different world from the chilly eight a.m. Communion when you don't need to talk to anyone!

There were these strengths at Corinth; but they had massive weaknesses too. Corinth is such an exciting church to study because their successes and failures are flashed before us in neon lights. Paul mentions four weaknesses which spoiled their Communions at Corinth, and which frequently apply today. These can make it possible for people to come out of the service worse off than when they went in (1 Cor. 11:17).

THEIR FAILURES AT CORINTH

First, their divisions (1 Cor. 11:18): 'When you assemble as a church, I hear that there are divisions among you,' says Paul, and tactfully adds, 'and I partly believe it.' Divisions are the fastest way to wreck a church. How can you eat the feast of unity if you are unreconciled with other guests? If that happens, you act a lie. And many churches are notorious for it, to our shame. There are divisions between older and younger outlooks in the congregation, both determined to have their way: divisions between social classes, between choir and congregation, unreconciled quarrels even in the same family. How does the Lord feel when we come to his table like that?

Second, their self-centredness (1 Cor. 11:21): 'In eating, each one goes ahead with his own meal, and one is hungry and another is drunk.' In Corinth this meant that the rich came early and ate and drank their fill, leaving little for the slaves who, perforce, joined them later. In modern congregations selfishness displays itself in other ways, not least in the individualistic conception of '*me* making *my* Communion' with little or no consideration for or integration with others.

Third, their irreverence (1 Cor. 11:27): 'Whoever . . . eats the bread or drinks the cup of the Lord in an unworthy manner will be guilty of profaning the body and blood of the Lord.' Strong words, but necessary. It is all too possible to drift into a Communion unprepared, to come to the Lord's table without repentance or forgiveness, and to treat the sacred emblems themselves with careless familiarity. The Communion should be a time of deep contrition and reverence.

Fourth, their compromise (1 Cor. 10:21): Paul stresses that they 'cannot drink the cup of the Lord and the cup of demons'. In Corinth they had not cut off the links with the old life. They still went into the trade guilds of the Temple of Apollo and took part in the idolatrous meals, feeling that there was nothing in all this idolatrous worship, so it must be all right (1 Cor. 8:1f.). This represented compromise at the deepest level, and the Lord is a jealous God who will not share his people with other deities. Whether or not they realised it, idolatry did make people vulnerable to forces which do not come from God: it still does. Playing with some form or other of the occult has made enormous inroads into Western society, including church people. Ouija boards, tarot cards, palm reading, spiritualism, not to mention white and black magic – these are more common among us than they have been for centuries. The demonic is not dead. It is active and dynamic. The eucharist is also active and dynamic. In 1 Cor. 11:29–30 Paul says, 'Anyone who eats and drinks without discerning the body eats and drinks judgment upon himself. That is why many of you are weak and ill, and some have died.' Whether by 'the body' he means the body of believers or the eucharistic body of Christ in the sacrament is not clear; what is clear is that compromise with idolatry in the Supper can have physical ill effects on those who do it.

PAUL'S GUIDELINES AT CORINTH

In this remarkable chapter the apostle gives no less than six guidelines for making the most of the Holy Communion. Their application is not confined to Corinth.

1. *Look back* (1 Cor. 11:23–4). 'The night when he was betrayed' was Passover night, and the Holy Communion is seen as the Christian Passover in 1 Cor. 5:7. It was the night of nights for the Jew, when he celebrated his nation's release from Egypt, the land of cruel bondage, doom and death. God delivered them when a lamb had been sacrificed, and its blood applied to the doorpost of every household. The lamb died in place of the firstborn, when God's destroying angel passed by. You were only safe if you were under the blood. That is the thrust of Exodus 12, and ever afterwards the Israelites recalled this night of momentous deliverance. The president at the Passover

meal would say down the ages (and still says), 'This is the bread of affliction which our fathers ate in the wilderness,' as he broke the unleavened cakes. Imagine, then, the electric atmosphere in the upper room as Jesus, presiding among that group of his friends, substituted these words for that age-old formula: 'This is my body which is for you.' He was pointing to a deliverance which made the Exodus pale into insignificance – deliverance from the guilt and doom and bondage of sin. No wonder Jesus left us no book as his memorial, but a feast, a new Passover, to celebrate his cosmic achievement on Calvary. There he, the Lamb of God, shed his precious blood to set captives free. At the eucharist the believer reiterates the fact that he personally appropriates that shed blood and all it has achieved. The service impels us to look back with gratitude.

2. *Look in* (1 Cor. 11:27–8). The Communion is a time for self-examination. Paul alludes to the hunt for leaven which was carried out on Passover night – and still is. Leaven, or yeast, is often a symbol of evil in the scriptures, because it is always swelling and seething up. In 1 Cor. 5:7 we read, 'Cleanse out the old leaven that you may be a new lump, as you really are unleavened.' No man takes a meal with filthy hands: he washes first. And no man should take the supper of the Lord without self-examination, repentance and cleansing. Repentance must be real. It is no good my repenting of cruel gossip if I intend to keep it up. The Ten Commandments and the Sermon on the Mount, together with our known weaknesses, form a valuable check-list for this useful if uncomfortable expedient of self-examination. It used to be stressed too much, maybe. Now, I fancy, it is used too little. We are invited to look within, in repentance.

3. *Look up* (1 Cor. 11:20). Paul insists that this is no ordinary meal: it is the Lord's supper. He provides it. We eat with him. He is the risen and ascended head of the table. This is no supper in memory of a dead hero, but in communion with a living Lord. Part of the mystery of this amazing sacrament is that we both feed *on* Christ and *with* Christ. He is the host who invites us to be his guests, and he

is himself the nourishment for our souls, the bread of life. One often finds it said in Catholic circles that the Communion or Mass is the food for the Christian life; in Protestant circles that the Bible is. Neither are right. Christ is our nourishment, and he alone. But he communicates himself to us both through the book and the supper, along with prayer and the fellowship of other Christians. Whether in prayer or Bible reading, or at the Communion itself, we need to look up to Christ to be fed.

4. *Look around* (1 Cor. 11:29). There is a horizontal dimension to the eucharist. That is plain from the whole context in 1 Corinthians 11, where some of the Corinthians are rebuked for their greed and selfishness at the meal. Possibly this is the meaning of eating and drinking 'without discerning the body'. One limb acting without regard to the other limbs causes havoc in the body. We are called to love one another and respect one another. Many churches have 'the Peace' or some equivalent, in which members of the congregation take time to greet each other, affirm each other and make up any quarrel that may exist. In any case, all come on a level to that table. All are equally his guests. Nobody has earned the right to be there: it is a free invitation arising from the unmerited love of the host. So there is no room for pride, and none for bad relations between members and the head or each other. Side by side men and women of whatever race, class and achievement stand or kneel and extend empty hands to receive the symbols of their redemption by Christ. It is a great time for looking round in fellowship.

5. *Look forward* (1 Cor. 11:26). 'As often as you eat this bread and drink the cup, you proclaim the Lord's death until he comes.' Each Communion service is a foretaste of heaven. It is a precursor of the messianic banquet, the marriage supper of the Lamb when his bride, the perfected church, will be united with him in joy for ever. In the midst of social disintegration, political danger or personal agony, this service invites us to lift up our heads, for our redemption draws nigh. It invites us to see the cross and resurrec-

tion, and the salvation springing from them, as the first instalment of God's future bliss for his people. It proclaims 'Our God reigns.' No wonder the early believers cried in their native Aramaic at the Supper of the Lord, '*Maranatha!*' It means 'O Lord, come!' It was the cry of aspiration from the believers who longed to be for ever with their Lord. It superbly expressed the forward look of the eucharist.

6. *Look outwards* (1 Cor. 11:26). 'As often as you eat this bread and drink the cup, you proclaim the Lord's death until he comes.' 'Proclaim' is another of the ambiguous words in which this memorable passage abounds. It may mean that in the eucharist we say, as it were, to God, 'Lord, we rely on the death of Christ Jesus and on nothing else.' In that sense we would proclaim it to God. But it also certainly means (for this is a very common Greek verb) that we proclaim it to men. I have often known people come to a living faith through being present at a Communion service. Nothing speaks more eloquently than the Communion of his death for us, and our need personally to appropriate its blessing.

But not only does the eucharist speak so eloquently and clearly of the gospel; it is also a goad in the service of that gospel. We are sent out from that service into the world as Christ's ambassadors. That is the probable meaning of its old Latin name, the Mass. '*Ite, missa est*' – 'Go, you have been sent.' The eucharist is battle rations for Christian warriors, not cream cake for Christian layabouts. Christian people are challenged, as they receive it, to go out and be his broken body here on earth for all the bleeding, needy people they meet. There are a couple of haunting words that re-echo through this passage: 'for you'. The Lord says to us, 'My body broken, my blood shed for you.' And as we receive in adoration and gratitude we are inspired to look a needy world in the face and say 'my body . . . for you.'

The Holy Communion is a many-splendoured thing.

CHAPTER FIVE

BODY LIFE

The Body of Christ, if coupled with the Spirit of Christ, reproduces something of the life of Christ in every church where this teaching and this power is taken seriously.

THE BODY OF CHRIST

The church is not a building, not a voluntary society, not an optional extra at the end of a busy week. It is the Body of Christ. And that is what Paul is at pains to instil into the minds of the Christians at Corinth. It is just as vital – and revolutionary – a concept today.

He speaks of 'the Body of Christ' in four ways: his physical body, his risen body, his eucharistic body, and his mystical body. All four are linked – not least the last two. 'The bread which we break, is it not a participation in the body of Christ? Because there is one bread, we who are many are one body, for we all partake of the one bread' (1 Cor. 10:16–17). Feeding on the body of Christ in the eucharist helps to unify the body of Christ which is the congregation at Corinth.

This is a mighty theme, and Paul gives full weight to it in 1 Corinthians 12. He does not say that the Church is like a body. He says that the church *is* the Body of Christ (1 Cor. 12:12, 27). It is a theme to which he reverts time and again.

In Romans 12 and 1 Corinthians 12 it is the interrelation of the members of that Body which primarily interests him. In Eph. 4:10–16 and Col. 1:18 he concentrates on the headship of Christ over that Body. The total image which emerges from these passages is gripping.

The Body means the visible expression of Christ. It is through our bodies that our ego is expressed. So it is with Christ. The only Christ men see is his people. Thus when Paul was persecuting the early Christians he heard on the Damascus road this question, 'Why are you persecuting *Me*?'

The Body means interdependence and harmony. No part has all the gifts. No part is readily dispensable.

The Body means that there is no room for pride on the one hand, or jealousy on the other. Still less is there room for independence.

The Body means that ministry is not the perquisite of the few but is the responsibility of every part. All churches should be devoted to the ideal of every-member ministry.

The Body means mutual respect between the members, as it operates through variety and unity. Unity is as crucial as diversity.

The Body owes its life and direction to the head, the brain which governs every movement and shows itself in every gesture.

The Body is not static. It grows in harmony, stature and usefulness. So must the Body of Christ grow in honesty, giving, depth, numbers and maturity.

'When each part is working properly,' cautions St Paul (Eph. 4:16). That's the rub. In most churches that is far from the case. They suffer various maladies in the Body of Christ.

Amputation from the Body is one of these. Members cut themselves off from really committing themselves to one another: they draw back from costly shared life together. It is easier just to go to eight o'clock . . . or not to go at all. Both amputated limbs and the remaining trunk lose out.

Elephantiasis in the Body is the most common of all

diseases. Some member, usually the minister, has grown to a size far greater than he ought to be. The result is that other parts are inhibited from making their contribution, and so he finds himself doing all sorts of tasks for which he is not fitted.

Atrophy in the Body is very common. Many members just sit there at a service and think that is all there is to the Christian life. There is no exercise, no muscle-building activity from such members. As a result even such strength as they have becomes atrophied. Like a man who has been lying in bed inactive for a month, they can barely stand if they try to get up.

Fractures occur all too often in the Body. Members fall out with one another and they blandly assume that nobody is harmed but themselves. This is far from the truth. Think of what agony for the whole of your body is caused by one broken toe. What must the living Head, Jesus Christ, feel about his Body, plaugued by multiple fractures?

Arthritis is another ailment all too common in our human bodies, especially old ones. And it is found in long-standing Christian bodies as frequently as in brand new assemblies. It is an abrasiveness, a grinding of bone upon bone. And it hurts. Of course, in a well-regulated body this does not happen. Bone does not grind upon bone, but upon a seating of gristle instead. The name of that gristle in the Body of Christ is love. 'Speaking the truth in love, we are to grow up in every way into him who is the head, into Christ, from whom the whole body, joined and knit together by every joint with which it is supplied, when each part is working properly, makes bodily growth and upbuilds itself in love' (Eph. 4:15f.).

If a church is to be an effective and true manifestation of Christ's life, it needs to work and pray for deepening unity and steady growth in truth and love.

THE SPIRIT OF CHRIST
The sort of church life we have been looking at is quite impossible without the Spirit of Christ. It simply can't be

done. And it was the Spirit of Christ that caused such a stir and division at Corinth. It still does . . .

Corinth was a richly gifted church in spiritual things. In almost the opening words of 1 Corinthians Paul thanks God for the grace given them in Christ, so that in every way they have been enriched in him. As a result there was plenty of evidence in their church of rather special manifestations of God's Holy Spirit. Some spoke with tongues. Some gave helpful prophetic messages. Some healed different types of illness. Some delivered people from demonic oppression. There was nothing dull about church life in Corinth.

The trouble was that those with these remarkable gifts became smug about it. They despised their less obviously gifted friends. They set themselves up as top-grade Christians with the other members of the congregation as 'also rans', if they were Christians at all . . . After all, *they* had received the blessing! *They* had been baptised in the Holy Spirit! Such was the situation which caused the Corinthians to write to Paul for his advice. He gives it in chapters 12–14 of 1 Corinthians.

To the surprise of the very gifted brethren at Corinth, the apostle does not agree with them. It is not only they, but all members of the Body who have been baptized by Christ's Spirit. 'For by one Spirit we were all baptized into one Body – Jews or Greeks, slaves or free – and all were made to drink of one Spirit (1 Cor. 12:13). Paul is very direct and very firm. All Christians, not just some specially gifted prophets or tongues speakers, are baptised in the Holy Spirit. It is the Spirit that enables one to make the most basic of all Christian affirmations, required at every baptism, that Jesus is Lord. 'No one speaking by the Spirit of God ever says . . . "Jesus is Lord" except by the Holy Spirit' (1 Cor. 12:3). Baptism by the Spirit is not some high-octane Christian experience but the basic necessity for being a Christian at all.

Once we are brought into God's family, the whole Trinity sets to work within us (1 Cor. 12:4–6, 'the same Spirit' . . . 'the same Lord' . . . 'the same God'). There is diversity in gifts but unity in their source, God. The three words Paul uses in these verses are helpful. There are varieties of love gifts, *charismata* (and therefore no room for pride). There are varieties of service, *diakonia* (that is what gifts are for). And there are varieties of workings, *energemata* (and so all Christian service must be undertaken in his energy, not our own). But behind it all is one God, active in and through the Body of Christ.

Paul then goes on to instance what some of these spiritual endowments might be. He mentions nine in 1 Cor. 12:8–11: three gifts of saying – tongues, interpretation and prophecy. Three gifts of doing – healing, exorcism, faith. Three gifts of knowing – discernment, knowledge, wisdom. I have discussed them extensively in *I Believe in the Holy Spirit*, and shall not do so again here. It is clear that he does not mean his list to be exhaustive. He offers a different list in verses 28–30 of this same chapter, a different list in Rom. 12:4–8, and a different list still in Eph. 4:11–12. His main point is that God is diversity-in-unity in his own being, and longs to see that diversity-in-unity reflected in Christ's Body, the church. There is a marvellous interweaving of three divine strands in this chapter's dealing with spiritual gifts. The Father places the gifts – and the limbs – within the Body (1 Cor. 12:6, 18, 24, 28). It is within the Son's Body that all are incorporated (1 Cor. 12:12, 13, 27). And it is the Spirit's joy to manifest himself through diversity-in-unity within that Body (1 Cor. 12:4, 7, 8–13).

And why all these gifts? Paul makes it plain that these gifts are not for the personal gratification of the recipients or to be used as a club to hit other Christians with. They are 'for the common good' (1 Cor. 12:7) or for 'building up the church' (1 Cor. 14:12).

THE BODY AND THE SPIRIT
The gifts of the Spirit are for the Body of Christ, which is exceedingly diverse (1 Cor. 12:14). The last half of this chapter is very important, but often neglected in modern discussion of spiritual gifts. What follows is directed to

three groups, those who feel inferior (1 Cor. 12:15–20), those who feel superior (1 Cor. 12:21–6), and finally to the whole church (1 Cor. 12:27–30).

Some feel inferior. They envy the gifts of other limbs in the Body, or they underrate their own. Paul gives them great encouragement. He tells them they are indeed in the Body, nourished by the same Spirit as those they look to with admiration or envy (1 Cor. 12:15). He tells them they are all necessary; is the eye not as important as the ear (1 Cor. 12:17)? He tells them they are special: God has chosen them and arranged them in the Body precisely as he saw fit (1 Cor. 12:18). They are all part of God's grand, harmonious design (1 Cor. 12:18).

Some feel superior. They are too big for their boots. So to them Paul gives a fourfold warning. There is no room for arrogance in their lives: all members of the Body are necessary (1 Cor. 12:22). There is no room for self-congratulation: God takes special care of the less gifted (1 Cor. 12:23). There is no room for dividing the Body: God has put it together (1 Cor. 12:25). There is no room for monopolising the limelight: otherwise the whole Body suffers (1 Cor. 12:26).

Paul ends with a word to the church as a whole. All gifts are to be accepted and welcomed, for they are God-given (1 Cor. 12:28). No man has them all; so jealousy, arrogance and independence are all equally inappropriate within Christ's Body. Now apply that to the 'haves', then to the 'have-nots', and then to the schismatics in the modern and emotive area of charismatic gifts! Is not St Paul highly relevant for the problems of today?

As each of us seeks to live our lives as vital limbs along with others in the Body of Christ, there are some lasting lessons to bear in mind from this remarkable chapter. I must neither despise nor be jealous of the gifts God has allotted to others. I must never limit God in what he may see fit to give me, nor lay down to him the gifts that I think he should bestow on me. I must remember that the Enemy divides while the Spirit unites members in the one Body.

55

Accordingly, I need to learn from Christians who are unlike me, not to consort exclusively with my friends. I need to ask the Holy Spirit to show me what gifts he has endued me with, and then resolve to use them for the good of the church. I must not remain content with what I have accomplished. I must 'earnestly desire the higher gifts', while remembering that Jesus' criterion for greatness was service. I will recall that as I serve in what is least, he will be preparing me to take on greater responsibilities later. I must never imagine that I have all the gifts: I need others in the Body, just as they need me. And I will seek to remember the way the chapter closes, pointing to the 'still more excellent way' of love, the crown of the Holy Spirit's gifts. Such is the way for Body life to grow in the church of God.

CHAPTER SIX

LOVE

Love is the greatest thing in the world. It is the life-blood within the Body of Christ. But this famous chapter, 1 Corinthians 13, is so familiar that we have become dulled to its message. It might be good, therefore, to put to it some questions.

WHAT IS THE MARK OF DIVINE INSPIRATION?

This was as live an issue then as now. The Hebrews and the Greeks both spoke with divided voice.

On the one hand, there was plenty of support for the view that the non-rational is the mark of the Spirit. The Old Testament gave some sanction to this view with Balaam, Samson, and Saul dancing like a dervish. So did some of the Greek writers. Plato had written in the *Phaedrus*, 'It is by *mania* [ecstasy due to inspiration] that the greatest blessings come to us', and again in the *Timaeus*, 'No one in possession of his *nous*, his rational self, has reached the divine exaltation'. The supreme example of non-rational possession was the prophetess at Delphi, 'the foaming mouthpiece of the god'.

On the other hand, it could be urged that the rational was the mark of divine inspiration. Socrates was the outstanding example of this emphasis in Greek philosophy, and there are places in the Old Testament where the link between the divine Spirit and rationality is strongly made. 'The Spirit of the Lord speaks by me, his word is upon my tongue' was David's claim (2 Sam. 23:2).

If we were to ask Paul what he thought was the supreme mark of the Spirit's presence and influence, whether it lay in the rational or non-rational elements of Christianity, I am sure he would rebut the dilemma. He tells us in this chapter that the greatest manifestation of God's Spirit is love. Love inspired the Father to send his Son. Love inspired the Son to give himself. And the Spirit pours the love of God the Holy Trinity into our hearts. *That* is the mark of divine inspiration.

WHY DOES THIS CHAPTER OCCUR HERE?
It seems at first sight out of place, sandwiched between a discussion of spiritual gifts and prophecy. But in fact it is vital to the argument of the three chapters. The Corinthians had written to Paul about spiritual gifts. He tells them the supreme spiritual gift is love (1 Cor. 12:31, 13:1). Just because God is love, those who claim to be in touch with him must embody something of his character. Love is the middle term between the gifts of the Spirit and the service of the world.

Paul is not saying that the alternative to gifts is love. Far from it. He is showing us that a still more excellent way to exercise gifts is in love. If love is your aim, you will not use your gifts for purely personal gratification; you will not flaunt your gifts at inappropriate times; you will not inhibit others from using their gifts by the misuse of your own.

HOW IMPORTANT IS LOVE?
Love is the essential ingredient in the use of those gifts he had been discussing in chapter 12.

The tongues man cannot do without it (1 Cor. 13:1). At Corinth they were trying to. They exercised their gift in a way which made others feel small. Such parading of the gift made it sound less the language of heaven than the clanging of an empty gong or the frenzied clashing of cymbals in the Cybele cult. Tongues without love is horrible. It concentrates on the sub-personal and non-ethical. It encourages pride. It is often divisive. It is wrongly seen as a gateway to power, whereas without love it can be the passport to chaos. Misuse of this lovely gift has wrecked many a church; just as unloving rejection of it has.

The knowledge man cannot do without it (1 Cor. 13:2). Whether it is the gift of prophetic knowledge that he prizes, or theological understanding, or deep insight into the mind of the Lord, knowledge without love is barren. Theological knowledge, academic knowledge, book knowledge: I do not disparage them. But without love they are a poverty-stricken abstraction, bones devoid of flesh.

The faith man cannot do without it (1 Cor. 13:2). How we admire the great heroes of the faith. But what their biographies often omit to tell us is the disaster of their family lives. The home was neglected, and the children rebelled. That is because even faith without love is worth nothing.

The public benefactor cannot do without it (1 Cor. 13:3). The millionaire may give his thousands away. The flower people may drop out of the rat race. But without the corresponding character, what is achieved? Our possessions will all have to be left behind one day; we will only take with us our characters. And they are created by love.

The martyr cannot do without it (1 Cor. 13:3). He makes the supreme sacrifice; perhaps (if the reading *kauthēsōmai* is right) by one of the most painful ways, being burnt. But unless it is accompanied by love, nothing is gained.

It is not what we know that matters. It is not how gifted we are that matters. It is not even what we do that matters. It is what we are that is crucial. If we believe that, it may induce some revisions in our lifestyle.

WHY IS LOVE SO IMPORTANT?
Because love is the heart of Jesus, and the supreme function of the Holy Spirit is to make us like him.

In the Old Testament God showed his Spirit breaking in

powerfully to our world, like the desert winds whistling through the gullies. 'The Spirit of the Lord came mightily upon him [Samson], and he tore the lion asunder as one tears a kid' (Judg. 14:6). It often seemed to be a case of sub-personal, naked, invading power.

In the Old Testament God's Spirit was for special people – the king, the prophet: not for the likes of you and me.

And in the Old Testament God's Spirit was all too easily lost and withdrawn, as Samson and Saul discovered to their cost.

But then Jesus came, Jesus the man filled with the Spirit, the one who would, after his resurrection, uniquely dispense the Spirit. And from Pentecost onwards these three limitations from Old Testament days were removed. The Spirit became available for all. The Spirit will never be withdrawn. And the Spirit is now revealed to us as fully personal, stamped with the character of Jesus himself. If we want to know what the Father is like, he is Christlike. If we want to know what the Spirit is like, he too is Christlike. So always the mark of the Spirit's fulness in a church or an individual is likeness to Christ. And that means love. If men do not see love in us, they will not see Jesus. That is why the supreme endowment of the Spirit is love.

HOW DOES IT SHOW?

It shows as the life of Jesus in us. In 1 Cor. 13:4–7 Paul quietly sets the love of Jesus over against the failings so apparent at Corinth. They claimed they were following the 'higher' way of spiritual experience. Jesus beckoned them to the 'lower' way, the way of the Servant, the path of love.

Love is patient (1 Cor. 13:4). The Corinthians were not. They were impatient for their rights in lawsuits, impatient for their chosen spiritual gifts.

Love is kind (1 Cor. 13:4). The word means generous. The Corinthians were not like that. The rich ate all the supper at the love feast before Holy Communion, so the poor slaves, when they arrived late, had none.

Love is not jealous (1 Cor. 13:4). Many at Corinth were jealous of their more talented friends.

Love does not make a parade of itself (1 Cor. 13:4). Unlike many at Corinth, it is shy and self-effacing.

Love does not grow puffed up with self-esteem (1 Cor. 13:4). Many at Corinth did, as they traded in their spiritual experiences.

Love does not dig in the bin of shame (1 Cor. 13:5). It covers sins over; it does not rake them up. But it was not that way at Corinth.

Love is unselfish (1 Cor. 13:5). Jesus was. But that was scarcely the most noteworthy characteristic of the Corinthians.

Love is not irritable (1 Cor. 13:5). The choleric, factious Corinthians had a lot to learn in this respect from Jesus Christ. Love abjures the sharp retort.

Love is not moody (1 Cor. 13:5) and does not brood over wrongs, real or imagined. Jesus didn't. Did they at Corinth?

Love does not revel in what is evil but rejoices in what is true (1 Cor. 13:6). That scarcely needs stating for Jesus: but it does not describe our conversation and reading matter, and I should be surprised if it did at Corinth.

Love can put up with everything (1 Cor. 13:7); loneliness, lack of encouragement, opposition, neglect. But the spiritual showmen at Corinth could not.

Love believes the best about people, not the worst.

Love, experienced now, is the firm platform for future hope.

Love endures whatever comes, without turning into cynicism (1 Cor. 13:7).

Love never gives up, like the love of Jesus on the cross. It is like an oak tree that stands firm.

HOW DOES LOVE WEAR?
Wonderfully well. For loving self-giving is the way of Jesus. It is the way of the Spirit. It is the life of heaven itself. When the day of all our earthly gifts is over, when all prophecy has

found its fulfilment, when tongues are taken up in the song
of the redeemed, when we know even as we are known,
when faith is swallowed up in sight, and hope is fulfilled in
utter possession by the Beloved – then love remains. The
redeemed in heaven will still be united in that glad self-
offering to the Lord and to the brethren which marked their
highest flights of spirituality on earth, when they were
brought by the Spirit into closest conformity with the love
of Jesus the Servant.

HOW DO WE STAND?

We shall not in the end be judged by our gifts or our
learning, but by our love, by our likeness to Christ. That,
among other things, is what the parable of the Sheep and
the Goats is teaching us. How shall we fare then?

How shall we fare when our church is judged in this light?
Much that we do as churches is totally irrelevant to the call
of love and the work of God's kingdom. We are preoccu-
pied with our own petty concerns and internal organisation.
We look like a Sunday School club for the pious: hence,
perhaps, the growth of many para-church organisations, in
frustration with the institutional church. Can our badge be
said to be love?

How shall we fare as individuals when judged by this
standard? Only what is done in love will bear inspection on
the last day. Is our life stamped by love? If not, we need to
change while there is time.

How shall we fare when our congregational life – the
gossip, the backbiting, the struggle for influence, the lazi-
ness, the hypocrisy – is judged in this light? How much do
we really love him? This is a difficult question to answer, as
John realised. So he gave us a helpful barometer: 'He who
does not love his brother whom he has seen, cannot love
God whom he has not seen' (1 John 4:20).

How shall we fare when our suffering is judged in this
light? A man like Bishop Wilson could pray for his torturers
as he rotted in a Japanese prison during World War Two,
and return afterwards to baptise some of them. But how do

62

we react towards those who make life hard for us? With love?

How shall we fare when our giving is judged in the light of love? The waste we contribute to, the opulence we enjoy while others starve, will rise up in testimony against us. So will the poverty of our actual giving to God's work.

How shall we fare when our caring is judged in this light? Not many churches are notable for their involvement with the hungry, the prostitutes, the alcoholics, the drug addicts.

How shall we fare when our evangelism is judged in this light? I heard not long ago of a community of Sawi headhunters who, seven years after their conversion, were supporting twenty-three missionaries from a church of some three hundred persons. Have we anything like their concern to reach the lost with the good news? On the whole we do not tell others because we do not love them enough.

We can do no better than ask God's Holy Spirit to shed abroad his own love in our hearts, and overflow from us to others (Rom. 5:5). 'Make love your aim . . . the greatest of these is love.'

CHAPTER SEVEN

WORSHIP

At first sight 1 Corinthians 14 seems to be a comparison and contrast between the merits of prophecy and tongues. But all the time Paul is thinking of the effect on the congregation, and it soon becomes plain that the real subject of this chapter is worship in the church at Corinth. I propose to extract six characteristics which Paul wanted to see in their worship, and discover their relevance despite the world of difference between their situation and our own. They lived in the first century, we in the twentieth. They were passionate Orientals, we cool Westerners. They were still a revolutionary movement in the making, while we mostly come from long-established churches blessed – and encumbered – with centuries of history and tradition.

Granted this very different context for the Corinthians and ourselves, let us look at the glimpse given in this chapter of an exciting, growing church at worship.

1. THE PLACE OF ORDER (1 Cor. 14:23, 29, 40)

It is not merely Anglicans who are concerned about order in the church. St Paul was as well. It would be mistaken to pit order against life. We should rather seek in our worship to combine life with order. 'Decently and in order' (1 Cor. 14:40) means just what it says. It does not indicate that things should be precisely the same every week. Within the ordered structure of most liturgical churches there is plenty of room for the informal and the topical to be inserted. There is adequate scope for flexibility. In churches that do not have a liturgical tradition there should be no problem – though there often is! But one thing is abundantly clear from this chapter. If spiritual gifts are to be used in worship, then discipline must go with them. There must be no tongues without interpretation – does that happen in most Pentecostal churches? There must be no men or women making an exhibition of themselves in the service – does that happen in most churches touched by the renewal? Gifts and discipline must go hand in hand.

2. THE PLACE OF PRAISE AND PRAYER (1 Cor. 14:15–17)

Every great movement of the Holy Spirit has been marked by song. Here Paul talks of two kinds of singing: singing in the Spirit, by which I take him to mean singing in tongues, and singing with the mind, that is to say normal singing. Psalms, hymns and spiritual songs were to be expected among believers who had been filled by the Spirit and were accordingly making melody to the Lord in their hearts (1 Cor. 14:26, cf. Eph. 5:18–19). We cannot doubt that heartfelt praise was one of the most striking characteristics of the early church. Typically, we find Paul and Silas, when thrown into prison at Philippi after a cruel whipping, singing hymns to God at midnight (Acts 16:25).

If we are to take this emphasis seriously for our own church life, it will demand some changes. It will mean a close rapport between the minister and the organist – and this does not always happen! It will mean that they plan and pray together over the music so that there is a wholeness about the complete service; but either will be prepared for a last-minute change should the mood of the service demand it. It will involve retaining many of the old favourites and blending with them new songs, many of them perhaps spontaneous creations from within the choir itself. This will demand a high degree of love, trust, prayer and fellowship among those leading the music. There may be singing while people are coming in or while they receive Holy Communion. Sometimes members of the congregation will be invited to choose the hymns. On occasion a considerable time will be spent in the praise of God, not resting content with the one statutory opening hymn. Singing in tongues may sometimes come as a climax to such an extended time of praise. Those who are musically gifted will be encouraged to help lead the worship, and a small orchestra may well form. Why should the organ be the only instrument thought fit to lead the worship of God? Why should one man do it all? Churches should give thought to appointing not organists but directors of music, whose task will be to gather together and exploit the musical talents of the people for the worship of the Lord.

Prayer is central to any Christian endeavour. Verse 15 of 1 Cor. 14 speaks of prayer in tongues and prayer in ordinary language. Neither is out of place in church. But if there is to be prayer in tongues it should either be under the breath (1 Cor. 14:28–9) or, if given out loud, should be interpreted (1 Cor. 14:27). Uninterpreted tongues are not edifying to anybody in the congregation, and St Paul forbids it.

The main thrust of Paul's advice is to pray with the spirit and also with the mind (1 Cor. 14:15). He wants prayer to be sincere, from the heart, and well informed. We have only to look at examples of his own prayers for the Corinthians (1 Cor. 1:1–9), the Philippians (Phil. 1:3–11), or the Colossians (Col. 1:9–14) to see the sort of thing he had in mind: deeply spiritual, practical, precise prayer, manifestly in line with the will of God. 'You also must help us by prayer,' he writes in 2 Cor. 1:11, 'so that many will give thanks on our behalf for the blessing granted us in answer to many prayers.' 'They long for you and pray for you,' was another of his comments (2 Cor. 9:14). Individual prayer, family prayer (1 Cor. 7:5) and prayer in church constituted top priority for Paul. If this is to become true of the modern church, a lot of care needs to be given to teaching on the subject. Ministers need to be known to be men of prayer. Prayer nights, prayer breakfasts and silent times of meditation need to be part of the life of the church. The way public prayers are led, the use of silence, the freedom for people to participate either in extempore or prepared prayers, expectant prayers for healing, and thanksgiving for answered prayers should be natural in any lively assembly of Christ's people. Alas, it is not always so. When activism dislodges prayer, blessing departs. The key to every great work of God which one has seen or read of is prayer. The secret of any really growing and spiritual church lies in prayer. And yet we are so slow to learn. A recent survey of the prayer habits of one great Western nation revealed the meagre average of two minutes a day for members at large, and three minutes a day for ministers!

3. THE PLACE OF PARTICIPATION (1 Cor. 14:6, 26)
The scale of participation envisaged in these two verses alone is considerable. A variety of people, a variety of contributions, a variety of spiritual gifts, but all with a common goal – to worship God acceptably. When that happens the outsider does sense that 'God is really among you' (1 Cor. 14:25). Congregations need to be participants, not an audience. In the old days, mystery plays, processions, social gatherings in church all had their place in enabling people to work together, and modern equivalents should be sought. But most of all there needs to be full participation in the regular worship of the church.

Why should we not do what the apostle suggests, and allow room for individuals to suggest a hymn, to share something God has revealed to them, to give a message in tongues with interpretation at a particular place in the service, or to give some message in prophetic vein? In this way the congregation may be edified. Of course there will be mistakes. Some people will think they are prophesying when they are doing nothing of the sort. There will be growing pains and some appalling gaffes. But if members of the congregation are maturing in love and in healthy self-criticism these problems will soon be ironed out, and the whole church will profit from the enlarged participation. In our own church this has been so, and now it does not matter if all the clergy are away: lay members of the congregation are well able to lead the worship and preach. Often teams go out from the church to other parts, and these may just as well be led by lay as by ordained members of the church. These are some of the benefits we have found through giving opportunity for a good deal of participation in the services – and we belong to an Anglican church which has its own fairly set liturgy. If it can be done there, it can be done anywhere!

Particularly when it comes to the sermon, there is no need for a monologue. Dialogue preaching is a valuable change sometimes. So is the place of testimony from members of the congregation. Drama can have an important part in worship and adds enormously to its colour and freshness. So does the judicious use of movement, when bodies no less than voices are used to the glory of God. Sometimes the scripture passage lends itself to a dramatic reading. The prayers may be led by several folk, and more than one can be involved in actually leading the service and reading the lessons. When the minister is asked to go and speak elsewhere, why should he not take with him two or three members of the congregation who can share in the ministry, to the blessing of all involved?

The place of participation is very important in worship. The one-man band is anathema.

4. THE PLACE OF JOINT LEADERSHIP (1 Cor. 14:29)

It is clear that no one person ran the worship at Corinth. There were several in a leadership role, as is plain from verse 29. This is in line with what we find elsewhere. Paul and Barnabas set up presbyters in the churches of Galatia (Acts 14:23) and we find shared leadership at Antioch (Acts 13:1f.) and elsewhere. Solo leadership seems to have been unknown. Presbyters always appear in the plural in the New Testament. This is not accidental. If a man is alone he is likely to be the more easily discouraged, threatened and lonely. He is likely to be the more ill-balanced and inadequate to cope with the wide-ranging demands of ministry. It is not good for a man to be alone in ministry. It is bad for him and bad for the church. We all need a supporting group.

'Ah,' you say, 'that is impossible in my situation. I am on my own.' You need not be. Is there no little group of spiritually minded people you could gather round you? What about a breakfast meeting on, say, Saturdays at seven a.m.? I know several churches that have found such a gathering of leading people in the church to be immensely beneficial. They have talked and prayed over different aspects of the life of the church. They have taken a share in appropriate action. They have grown in so doing. They have encouraged each other: they have shared the load. It is perfectly possible, even in a very small church, to build up a small team round the minister – if he wants it. Some ministers feel threatened by the very idea. Some feel it will detract from their professionalism. Some are terrified at letting others come too close. But the value of shared ministry was manifest at Corinth. Not one person but a recognisable group might be expected to engage in prophetic ministry (1 Cor. 14:29); St James thinks of a similar group taking part in the healing ministry (Jas. 5:14); while at Antioch five men of very different gifts and backgrounds came together to lead the church in worship and outreach (Acts 13:1). This is surely a cardinal principle in any church which intends to deepen fellowship and grow. The leaders must model the type of fellowship they want to see reflected in the congregation. Unless there is a sharing of life among the leaders it is hardly realistic to expect much depth of fellowship among the congregation. But when this becomes common in fellowship groups throughout the church as well as in the leadership, then worship takes on a new dimension.

5. THE PLACE OF EDIFICATION (1 Cor. 14:19, 26, 31, 40)

Paul was very concerned that the church should be built up in knowledge, love and service. In these services of worship the Old Testament was used a good deal, probably the words of Jesus as well, certainly letters from Paul and other Christian leaders, and short prophetic messages given during the service (1 Cor. 14:19, 31). He wants all to learn, all to be encouraged and consoled (1 Cor. 14:3, 31).

Many modern congregations have almost no understanding of the Old Testament or the Pauline letters, and would have apoplexy if anyone were to give a prophetic message! Most modern Christians can scarcely be said to be well informed on the contents of their faith and the reasons for holding it. So Christian leaders would do well to share the concern of St Paul that members of the congregation are edified.

Various methods of learning have commended themselves in recent years. There is a value in sometimes having questions handed in to be dealt with in the sermon. There is value in having a lunch together afterwards with the opportunity to discuss what has been said in the sermon and its application in the life of the church. If there are fellowship groups in the parish they could well examine some further aspect of what had been preached on the previous Sunday, and apply it to their area and their Christian witness within it. There is value in setting up appropriate groups for agnostics, for seekers, for new Christians, and for those wanting training in Christian leadership, marriage, or mission. There should be training for leaders of organisations in the church, and for any lay pastors who emerge with gifts that the congregation wishes to recognise and benefit from. One of the most effective ways of learning is to engage in practical faith-sharing trips outside the parish. This brings growing experience and tremendous joy. Edification is one of the prime functions of Christian worship and fellowship.

6. THE PLACE OF EVANGELISM (1 Cor. 14:24-5)

Paul was very anxious that the unbeliever or outsider entering a service of Christian worship should have the sense that God is among them, and should be drawn towards him. He was concerned to make the church alive for mission, so that 'if an unbeliever or outsider enters, he is convicted by all, he is called to account by all, the secrets of his heart are disclosed; and so, falling on his face, he will worship God and declare that God is really among you' (1 Cor. 14:24-5). I have known services like that. But many churches today are not looking in this direction at all. They do not expect outsiders to come in, except at great festivals. There is little sense that God is really in the midst. Many churches do not expect unbelievers to be converted, and they would hardly know what to do with them if they were. The church is seen as a raft to cling to for survival, rather than a trawler out to catch fish. But Jesus Christ is and always has been in the fishing business. Peter was sent out to catch men as well as to feed sheep. And so are his followers in the modern world. In most parts of the globe other than Western Europe the churches are slanted towards evangelism and outreach. They do have the outsider at least in the back of their minds, and they expect unbelievers to be attracted, won to the faith, and edified. We need to recover that sense of expectancy. We need to so give ourselves to the worship of God that his glow is seen in our midst. We need to rid ourselves of the tyranny of the clock, and be prepared if need be to spend some considerable time in worship.

Moreover, we need to have a few services in the year when we specially set out to explain God's way of salvation to those who are not normally worshipping members of the congregation. Such occasions will need to be carefully prepared. The members of the congregation will need to know in good time, so that they can invite their friends. The whole thing needs to be bathed in prayer. All this takes time and trouble to bring about, but it is eminently worth while. The steady flow of new Christians into the church saves the congregation from loss of faith and expectancy, and from falling into a rut. It calls for constant self-scrutiny in areas of music, prayer, preaching, testimony and the like. But it needs to be part of every healthy church's life. For, as William Temple succinctly put it, 'the church is the only society in the world which exists for the benefit of non-members' – but it is very apt to forget that fact.

Many churches in the developing nations are already putting into practice most of the principles of worship which Paul teaches in this chapter. But the same cannot be said for the staid churches of the Western world, encumbered as we are by our traditions, imprisoned in our professionalism and divided by our denominationalism. We believe in order: but where is that spiritual vitality which made Paul's teaching on order essential? To be honest, we do not know much of heartfelt praise and earnest prayer. We are not noted for congregational participation. We know little if anything of joint leadership. The level of informed understanding in most congregations shows that, whether or not edification has been attempted, it has scarcely succeeded. And our churches seem to have nothing to offer the outsider: so he does not come. It would be a great mistake to see the injunctions in this chapter as simply referring to a primitive and undisciplined congregation in a missionary situation. They pose a highly contemporary challenge to a great deal of what goes on in church and chapel Sunday by Sunday in the twentieth century.

CHAPTER EIGHT

PROPHECY

Granted that worship is the underlying theme in 1 Corinthians 14, it must not be thought that I want to duck out of the more controversial issue dealt with there, namely prophecy. Few subjects are more calculated to stir surprise and caution in the church. If we consider it at all, we are liable to confine prophecy either to men like Isaiah or else to exceptionally perceptive moderns such as Solzhenitsyn or Temple. But that is not what Paul meant in 1 Corinthians 14.

WHAT IS CHRISTIAN PROPHECY?
Corinth was alive with charismatic Christianity, some of it splendid and some of it wild. They were infatuated with the gift of tongues, and had written to Paul about it. Paul replies, in effect, in chapter 12, 'You are all one body; different and complementary limbs, with different gifts endowed by the Holy Spirit. How dare one limb boast against another?' In chapter 13 his point is, 'You may speak with the tongues of men and angels, but if you do not have love, you are nothing.' This leads naturally into 1 Cor. 14:1, 'Make love your aim, and earnestly desire the spiritual gifts, especially that you may prophesy.' Why so? Because prophecy is not, like tongues, incomprehensible without

interpretation (1 Cor. 14:6–12). It is clear to all who hear it. And prophecy is not, like tongues, of value only to the individual (1 Cor. 14:2). It is for the church. For these two reasons Paul gives preference to prophecy over tongues. But what is it?

Prophecy is neither bizarre nor ecstatic. It is a perfectly intelligible word from the Lord through a member of his Body inspired by his Spirit, and is given to build up the rest of the Body. It is a message which the speaker does not make up. It is borne in upon him. He has to speak it out. And it is an act of faith. He or she does not normally know how it will end, only how it must begin . . .

We must remember that prophecy had been dead for centuries in Israel. But there was a great new flowering of it when Jesus Christ appeared – Mary, Simeon, Anna, Zacharias, John the Baptist, and supremely Jesus himself. He was the prophet like Moses (Matt. 21:11, John 6:14, Acts 3:22), the one who came to fulfil not only the law but the prophets in his own person. And the gift of prophecy was not removed when Jesus died. At Pentecost Joel 2:28 was fulfilled, 'I will pour out my spirit on all flesh; your sons and your daughters shall prophesy' (Acts 2:18). Interestingly enough, the concluding words, 'and [they] shall prophesy' are not in Joel. They are a Christian gloss. But they show clearly how the New Testament writers saw prophecy as a mark of the Spirit and of the new age. It may be helpful to glance at what prophecy is and what it is not.

First, prophecy is very widespread in the New Testament. Civilised men like Silas and wild men like Agabus had this gift. So did mystics like the author of Revelation and intellectuals like Paul. The Thessalonians are told not to despise it. Philip the evangelist had four prophesying daughters whose fame became legendary. You find prophets at Rome, Antioch, Jerusalem and in the churches of Asia.

Second, prophecy is highly valued in the New Testament. Prophets rank after apostles in the various lists of ministries (e.g. Eph. 2:20, 1 Cor. 12:28). They are equal to the apostles because both are agents of revelation, but subordinate to the apostles because they cannot go behind them to an independent interpretation of Jesus. The apostolic witness defines the faith.

Third, prophecy is very varied in the New Testament. It could come from one man or woman (1 Cor. 11:4f.) or from a prophetic group (Rev. 10:7, 22:6). It could come as prediction, encouragement, teaching, mysterious language, picture (as in the subapostolic prophetic writer, Hermas), use of scripture, or testimony to Jesus (Rev. 19:10). It could be used for edification or evangelism (1 Cor. 14:3, 24). But it was always intelligible speech, inspired by the Holy Spirit.

Now for three things prophecy is not.

First, it is not the equivalent of scripture. Prophecy is a particular word for a particular congregation at a particular time through a particular person. Scripture is for all Christians in all places at all times. That is the difference.

Second, it is not the same as preaching or teaching. In Paul's churches a woman was not permitted to teach but was permitted to prophesy (1 Cor. 11:5, 14:34). There is a clear distinction in 1 Cor. 12:29. Of course, one might move from teaching into prophecy, but the two are distinct.

Third, it did not die out after New Testament times. It has appeared spasmodically throughout church history. Prophets were much honoured in the second and third centuries, and were also evaluated with a praiseworthy caution. Thus a prophet might order a meal when in the Spirit . . . but he must not himself eat it! The unknown Catholic writer against Montanus is clear that 'the prophetic charisma will last to the end of the age throughout the church' (Eusebius, *H.E.* 5:17).

WHAT IS THE GOOD OF CHRISTIAN PROPHECY?

First, it is plain from 1 Cor. 14:4, 5, 12, 26 that prophecy is addressed to the church. It is not an ego trip by the person concerned.

Second, prophecy has a positive role (1 Cor. 14:3). It is

given to build up the church (*oikodomē*), to encourage the church (*paraklēsis*), to whisper in the church's ear (*paramuthia*) and to aid the church in outreach (1 Cor. 14:24–5). Prophecy does not rant. It is for the 'benefit' (1 Cor. 14:6) of God's people.

Third, prophecy may come in a variety of ways. I will illustrate them from personal experience to bring out what is meant.

Prophecy may come as a 'revelation', a picture revealed to a church member (1 Cor. 14:26). One such picture, received during a time of ministry, showed a barn with a group in it and a tree outside. A person being ministered to at once recognised it as a spot in which years ago she had unwittingly become involved with an occult circle, and it was clear in what way she needed to be helped.

Prophecy may come with a word of knowledge, an insight from God into the situation (1 Cor. 14:25). One bishop, ministering in our church to a man who confessed pride, said 'Nonsense, you are consumed with fear.' He was, and crumpled to the floor. The fear was immediately dealt with.

Prophecy may come as teaching (1 Cor. 14:22). One such prophecy brought immediate clarification and direction to our Church Council about a major project we had been discussing inconclusively. After the prophecy there was unanimity about the way to proceed.

Prophecy may be a very brief utterance. Thus in Haggai 1:13 all the prophet said was, 'I am with you, says the Lord' and sat down! But it was just what they needed. Do not despise the short word of encouragement.

A prophetic message may come through tongues and interpretation (1 Cor. 14:5): as when in Norway recently this message came to them through tongues and interpretation. 'Lay down your activities and seek me in silence. I need to have you silent so that you can receive from me what you need but cannot receive while you are so busy. And take care of the new song. I need your new song.' This message was heard, both in tongue and interpretation, by a woman who had been deaf for years and became deaf again immediately afterwards. There is multiple attestation to this fact: it happened in August 1979, and I personally met several people who had witnessed the event. It is of course plain from 1 Cor. 14:5, 13 that tongues and interpretation are the equivalent of prophecy.

Prophecy may come through scripture. We should not be sceptical of a prophecy couched in very biblical terms. The Book of Revelation is a prophecy (Rev. 1:3) but it contains over four hundred citations from the Old Testament. We may find ourselves directed to some suprising verse of scripture that proves invaluable. When praying for Dr Graham in his 1980 visit to Oxford some people in Scotland were led to a strange reference in the New English Bible (a version which they did not normally use). It was 1 Chr. 4:10, '"I pray thee, bless me and grant me wide territories. May thy hand be with me and do me no harm, I pray thee, and let me be free from pain." And God granted his petition.' Little did they realise how apt it was: he had fallen and broken some ribs. Their letter was a great encouragement and God took the pain from Dr Graham's broken ribs very soon after that.

A colleague of mine was drawn to Exodus 3:5 during a session with someone who had been deeply in the occult. 'Put off your shoes from your feet, for the place on which you are standing is holy ground.' The shoes were removed from the person involved, and the feet washed in holy water. That proved to be the climax of a deliverance which remains good today.

HOW DO YOU TEST CHRISTIAN PROPHECY?
The passage in 1 Corinthians 14 abounds in wise criteria.

First, does it glorify God (1 Cor. 14:25)? If the so-called prophecy glorifies the speaker, or a church or denomination, take leave to doubt it.

Second, is it in accord with scripture? In verses 37f. Paul reminds the prophets in Corinth to obey scriptural guidelines. They are not the only pebbles on the beach, and they must recognise that what he, Paul, is writing to them is a command from the Lord. See also Deut. 13:1–3.

Third, does the supposed prophecy build up the church (1 Cor. 14:5)? Of course, a message can build up even if it is rather disturbing. But does edification result all round? If not, it is unlikely to come from God.

Fourth, is it spoken with love (1 Cor. 14:1)? Prophecy is, after all, one of God's love gifts.

Fifth, does the speaker submit to the judgment and consensus of others (1 Cor. 14:29)? Or is he authoritarian and unteachable? Supposedly prophetic messages can be self-induced or satanic, and humility is a mark of authenticity.

Sixth, is the speaker in control of himself (1 Cor. 14:32)? Prophecy, like tongues, is neither ecstatic nor uncontrollable. Order is one of the signs of God's presence.

Seventh, is there too much of it (1 Cor. 14:29–30)? The longer a man (or several in succession) goes on the more likely he is to have confused his own ideas with God's word.

From other passages of scripture we learn to look at the life of the man professing prophetic gifts: if the tree is sound, so is the fruit likely to be. We are also encouraged to look at the man's relationships with his church leaders. If he is not attuned to them, God is unlikely to be at work. And finally we are bidden to look at the outcome of predictive prophecy. If it does not take place, God was not behind it (Deut. 18:22).

REQUIREMENTS FOR CHRISTIAN PROPHECY
It is perhaps worth pointing out that there are four major requirements which Paul alludes to here, if we are to expect to see a prophetic ministry in our churches today.

First, we must expect it, pray for it, and welcome it when it comes. We are told to desire prophecy (1 Cor. 14:1, 39). If we are determined not to have it at any price, then God is unlikely to give it to us.

Second, we must be obedient to God (1 Cor. 14:37f.). God gives his Spirit to those who obey him (Acts 5:32). The

78

person launching out in prophecy must obey the initial promptings of the Spirit, even though he or she is shy and does not know where it will end. The church must be obedient in sifting, assessing and then implementing what is offered (1 Cor. 14:29). If we do not obey the Lord, we can expect no further light . . . and probably no further prophecy.

Third, worship is the atmosphere most conducive to prophecy. It is so in this chapter, and in Acts (13:1f.). When our eyes are fixed on the Lord in worship, it is easy for him to speak.

Fourth, we must all make love our aim (1 Cor. 14:1). That is the really vital climate in which prophetic gifts can emerge and flourish. Love will be welcoming towards embryonic prophecy. Love will be forgiving when mistakes are made. Love will bind those with this gift and those without it into an interdependent unity. If the gifts of the Spirit are ever set against his supreme grace, the imparting of God's own love to our hearts, the gifts themselves will become ugly, and the congregation useless to the Lord.

It would be very easy to assign all such talk of prophecy to the lunatic fringes of the Christian church. If we do that, we shall, however, be the poorer, and we shall be quenching the Spirit. Paul was emphatic on this point. 'Do not quench the Spirit, do not despise prophesying,' he wrote (1 Thess. 5:19). Prophecy is one of the gifts of God to his Body, and he means us to use it. If we obey Paul's injunction, 'Make love your aim, and earnestly desire the spiritual gifts, especially that you may prophesy,' then we can expect to see the gift gently and tentatively emerging in one or more members of the congregation. They will be shy and hesitant, especially to start with. It will probably begin in a small meeting where there is a high level of mutual trust. It may well start through some mental picture coming to a member during a time of worship and silent adoration. If he or she has the courage to share it with the people, and if it really comes from God, then at once it will be seen to be relevant. Somebody will be helped by it, and will at once say so. In this way the group will be encouraged, and so will the person to whom the picture was given. And next time there will be just a little more confidence all round. If love flows, if mistakes are expected and understood, if the tests outlined above are applied, the dangers inherent in this sensitive gift will be largely avoided, and its real blessings will become a very positive boon to the congregation.

Part Two

Problems for the Members

CHAPTER NINE

INTELLECT

Corinth was an intellectual place, and rated the mind very highly. It had replaced Athens not only as the provincial capital of Greece but also as the intellectual centre. It was the natural bridge between Eastern and Western Mediterranean. Travelling teachers continually passed through. They taught wisdom. They were clever, logic-chopping men. They charged big fees. And Paul and Sosthenes must have appeared to many Corinthians in a similar light.

This was a misconception which Paul is at pains to destroy speedily. In the first four chapters of 1 Corinthians he makes three trenchant points.

First, the gospel is not wisdom in the accepted sense. On the contrary, it is, in the world's eyes, folly. And yet it is through this 'folly', revealed in the crucifixion of Jesus, that God determined to save believers. True, there is a Christian wisdom, but the Corinthians have a long way to go before they reach it: they are as yet totally worldly (1 Cor. 1:18f., 2:6, 3:1).

Second, the evangelists are not teachers of wisdom, like the travelling sophists. That view of them is at once too high (it gives them a position of their own, independent of God whose mouthpiece they are) and too low (it subjects them to the Corinthians' judgment). Of course, it pleases the

Corinthians to think of their leaders in this light: it ministers to their own self-esteem as they boast (and contend) about great names (1 Cor. 2:1–6, 3:18–23).

Third, the Corinthians need to revise their estimate of their own position. They are not judges over their ministers, as they imagine. They should rather consider the judgment they themselves will have to face, and be prepared to become fools, by this world's standards, so that they may become wise. Their duty is not to judge, but to emulate the apostles and the Saviour in suffering (1 Cor. 4:1–13). For all their emphasis on the intellect at Corinth they had got it wrong.

THEY FAILED TO APPRECIATE THE LIMITATIONS OF THE INTELLECT

We could get nowhere without our minds, but our minds, unaided, cannot solve every issue. Paul points out three areas of limitation in the intellect.

First, it cannot reach through to God. What is more, God never intended that it should, or trust would be unnecessary (1 Cor. 1:21). Moreover intellectuals could be unbearably arrogant. 'Can you find out the deep things of God?' was the question put to Job (Job 11:7) and the answer was clearly 'No'. God is, by definition, much bigger than our puny intellects. To be sure, there are some clues that my intellect can grasp, some facts it can latch on to. The fact that there is a world at all . . . the fact of design and order in it . . . the fact of personality and intellect . . . the fact of moral and aesthetic values . . . the fact of conscience . . . the fact of a religious awareness among every known culture and tribe in the world: all these things make it more reasonable to believe in a Creator than in mere randomness. But we remain with no more than probabilities. And Paul is saying, in effect, 'How could it be otherwise? How can you take in the Eternal? Unless he discloses himself you will never find him out.' That is precisely the thrust of 1 Cor. 2:9, 10. Professor C. E. M. Joad, after a lifetime of atheism, wrote in *Recovery of Belief* 'The nature of the spiritual world must remain unknown by reason. Intellect can light up only a small area of the universe.' In other words, it takes God to reveal God. And that, Paul believes, is what God has done.

Second, the unaided intellect cannot understand the cross (1 Cor. 1:18–19). There were then, as now, two slightly different types of intellectual approach to matters of religion. The first we might call the approach of the pure intellectual. The philosopher in the best traditions of Greek thought was looking for broad principles of universal applicability. The cross was nothing of the sort. It was not a universal but a particular, and a sordid one at that. How could a single execution in history have such tremendous significance as the Christians were claiming? The other type was the more argumentative intellectual, whose attitude is always 'Prove it to me'. He is looking for a compulsive sign, a mark of power. To him the cross was either no sign at all, or a sign of weakness and failure. Of course, no sign will compel if you are determined not to accept it; no evidence will be beyond cavil. In the days of his flesh Jesus was unable to give a compelling sign of who he was to those determined to reject him. He himself was the sign, and inevitably therefore could be construed in two ways. So could his cross. To the outward eye, here was weakness and defeat: to the inner eye, this thing was dynamite and dealt with human guilt, explained human suffering and pointed, through the resurrection, to human destiny.

Third, the unaided intellect finds it extremely difficult, well nigh impossible, to accept the gospel (1 Cor. 1:21). For human intellect is proud. It wants to prove itself, to show how fine a thing it is. It is most reluctant to accept grace. It is inimical to the whole principle of trust. Reason stands by itself, and wants no help from revelation.

It is for this reason that St Paul concentrates on Jesus Christ. 'We preach Christ crucified,' he insisted (1 Cor. 1:23). Let them wrestle with Jesus and his death: they would find there a focus for intellectual integrity that would enable them to look at the whole of life entire and unafraid.

For God has revealed himself in that Jesus and that cross. They will bear any scrutiny.

THEY GAVE WAY TO ABUSE OF THE INTELLECT

Here again there are three dangers which stare us in the face. Each had become a reality at Corinth.

Overemphasis on the intellect can so easily lead to arrogance. This was a major weakness with the Corinthians. 'Let no one deceive himself. If any one among you thinks that he is wise in this age, let him become a fool that he may become wise. For the wisdom of this world is folly with God' (1 Cor. 3:18–19). This is very evident when one looks back a generation. Time and again those who were the last word among the intellectual élite a generation ago are now seen to have been wildly mistaken – but in their own day, they would have none of it.

Overemphasis on the intellect can sometimes lead to valuing form more than content. That was certainly the case at Corinth, and it has been known in many of the parliaments of the world. In 1 Cor. 1:17 there is a reference to *sophia logou*, a wisdom or skill with words, which appealed enormously to the Greek mind. It stands in striking contrast to the reversal of those words in 1 Cor. 12:8. Here one of the gifts of God's Holy Spirit is a *logos sophias*, a word or message arising from wisdom. Content has taken over from form. Heresy does not improve by being well written or golden tongued. It is all too easy to be bewitched by brilliance.

Furthermore, overemphasis on the intellect can lead to division. It did at Corinth (1 Cor. 1:12f., 3:1–4). This is a thoroughly contemporary phenomenon, not least in political and religious circles. In the Christian church this is particularly deplorable and foolish. Why should the Corinthians stick to one man when there are several there to help them (1 Cor. 3:5)? Why should they glory in men when it is God who gives any spiritual growth (1 Cor. 3:6)? Why should they set one leader against another when they all have a common aim (1 Cor. 3:9)?

Abuse of the intellect is dangerously easy to fall into. It is a perilous disease to contract, for the Almighty says, 'I will destroy the wisdom of the wise, and the cleverness of the clever I will thwart' (1 Cor. 1:19).

THEY MISSED THE TRUE PLACE OF THE INTELLECT

It begins with the fear of the Lord. 'God chose what is low and despised in the world, even things that are not, to bring to nothing things that are, so that no human being might boast in the presence of God. He is the source of your life in Christ Jesus, whom God made our wisdom, our righteousness and sanctification and redemption; therefore, as it is written, "Let him who boasts, boast in the Lord"' (1 Cor. 1:28–31). 'Yet among the mature we do impart wisdom, although it is not a wisdom of this age' (1 Cor. 2:6). Wisdom will not bring you to God, but once you reach God he does give you spiritual wisdom. You receive a unified frame of reference. You see that there is one God, and the whole universe is sustained by his power and love. You see Jesus not as some Hindu *avatar* but as the cosmic Christ, the alpha and omega, the principle of coherence in the universe, the one in whom are hid all the treasures of wisdom and knowledge. You see him as the truth about God and man. You take all that is good or beautiful or true, wherever you find it, as rays of light from the Sun, Jesus Christ. You see the wholeness of human life and history held in God's hands. You see man as God's vicegerent in the world. You see time as contained in eternity, this life as preparation for the next. All this is poles apart from the secular perspective where this world is all there is, happiness is our only good, and reality is confined to what we perceive with our senses.

The fear of the Lord is indeed the beginning of wisdom. It is the perspective which makes all else fall into place. Thus when an atheistic scientist says to us, 'There is no gap for God's intervention in the direct chain of descent from early hominids to modern man,' we shall reply, 'We do not look for God in the gaps of scientific knowledge. We see him as the Lord of the whole universe, without whom there could be no development and no knowledge at all.' Even if there were complete continuity of physical development, that would not preclude the discontinuity of spiritual nature between men and animals. To use a simple analogy: the proportion of gas to air in a burner may be increased gradually and continuously until the mixture suddenly sustains a flame. When this happens we have a new thing, with a dynamic all its own, and with nothing corresponding to it in the earlier stages.

In another helpful analogy Professor Donald Mackay sees the world not as a machine but as a work of art. He likens it, not to a painting (that would be too static) but to a television system. The controller brings the picture into being by producing a rapid succession of sparks of light on the television tube. From those sparks of light the pictures are formed. The world he thus brings into being is not static but dynamic and able to change at his dictate. If he were to cease his activity, the result would not be chaos but darkness: it would simply cease to be. For he holds the scene in being. God's relation to our world may be illuminated somewhat by this model. Almighty God is the controller of the whole system who is never capricious but always deeply consistent. That is where you find the deepest harmony between the Christian faith and the scientific attitude. Both depend on the rationality and consistency of the ultimate reality behind our world. Both see faith not as credulity but as commitment to where the evidence points, however inconvenient it may be.

The true place of the intellect is not only to begin with the fear of the Lord but to concentrate on the revelation of the Lord (1 Cor. 2:9–10, cf. 1 Cor. 1:18, 31). We are not left to rely on unaided intellect. We have something to work on and apply. This is God's revelation, in nature, in scripture and supremely in Christ. If by definition the finite cannot exhaust the significance or pierce the infinite, then it is only common sense to immerse ourselves in the self-disclosure

God has given us in his two books of nature and scripture. Ours is an age which overvalues modernity. As Harry Blamires put it tartly, 'Unfortunately it is assumed that God rates human scholars in an order of preference based on inverted chronology.' We need to keep coming back to Christ, the source of all wisdom and knowledge. When theological students tell me that they are losing their faith, I reply that there is no need for it, so long as they remember that all truth (provided it really is true) is God's truth and cannot possibly harm them. Let them remember that their faith is placed in a person not in a doctrine or a text, and that the Christ they worship and proclaim is the source, the goal, and the upholder of the universe. Provided they remain humble before God, study the biblical testimony to the Beyond who came into the midst, and remain sensitive to truth, active in service and involved in worship, they cannot go far astray. But if they surrender to intellectual dualism and the secularist presuppositions of many modern writers who have no fear of God before their eyes, it is hardly surprising if their Christianity shrinks to the smile of the Cheshire cat after the animal itself has vanished.

Despite his conviction that the Old Testament could only fully be understood in the light of Christ, Paul held it in deepest reverence. He was convinced that the new truth in Christ was concealed in prediction, allegory and type in the Old Testament. For both came from the God who has disclosed himself to them. That is why in 1 Cor. 2:9–16 he lays such stress both on the scriptures and on the Spirit. He longs for them to wrestle with the scriptures, secure in the aid of the Spirit who inspired them. Only God can reveal God; and he has done so. He has inspired the apostolic writers to bear their irreplaceable testimony to Jesus in words taught by the Holy Spirit (1 Cor. 2:13). Note what the apostle is saying. Not merely the sentiments but the very words are chosen by the Spirit: 'We impart this in words not taught by human wisdom but taught by the Spirit.' In scripture we have a sufficient revelation from God. And we approach it using our minds to the full, 'comparing spiritual things with spiritual'. There is nothing wooden or cramping about assigning supremacy to scripture. We have to exercise our minds on it. But we are freed thereby from the paralysing effects of scepticism and the weathercock changes of theological fashion.

Finally, the true place of the intellect is gradually to be transformed into the Christian mind, the mind of Christ (1 Cor. 2:16). The indwelling Christ renews our minds as we seek the Christian perspective of God who is active in and throughout human affairs, and steep ourselves in the Christian resources of the scriptures. Gradually we develop an outlook, a judgment informed by Christ himself. We arrive at an integrity in our world view. This is the Christian wisdom of which Paul spoke in 1 Cor. 2:6. But it is not imparted for our own gratification alone: it is intended to be at the service of others. The pupil does not exist for the sake of his teacher: rather, the reverse is true (1 Cor. 3:21–2). If, then, the teacher of the faith exists for the benefit of those he serves, he has a responsibility to develop the mind of Christ in them. In our own intellectual climate, which exaggerates the place of analysis and compartmentalises knowledge, he will find it crucial to stress that Christ is the principle of coherence in every department of life. And Christ offers to develop his mind, his way of approaching things, in those who follow him. He is concerned to remake the intellect, which is part of the image of God in us, but has, in common with all our other faculties, been affected by the Fall. He, the source and goal of all knowledge, will shine his light on us more and more if we genuinely covet his mind on every issue in our lives.

CHAPTER TEN

FREEDOM

In ancient Corinth freedom was as electric a word as *Uhuru* has been in Africa during the past few decades. Imagine yourself a proletarian on Corinth's waterfront; a prostitute in Corinth's temple; a butcher in Corinth's meat market. And you come to Christ. You see him as a cult god, rather like in the Mysteries, but of course infinitely greater. You have the Spirit within you. You have tasted the powers of the new age. You have received remarkable gifts – knowledge, prophecy, tongues. You are already full (1 Cor. 4:8). You have already entered into your reign. You are free. You sit in judgment on your teachers. After all, are you not initiates in the heavenly sphere? Your good things are realised in the here and now: that is one of the reasons why you cannot bear any doctrine of the resurrection – which reserves some of those good things till later. You have equality with every Christian brother and spouse and master, first in the congregation and then in daily life in the city. 'All things are lawful' (1 Cor. 10:23) you cry. You have freedom, and freedom is a very heady wine.

So why should a woman keep silent in the congregation if the Spirit has come upon her? Why should a slave consent to be dependent on a Christian master? Why should prophets and those with other spiritual gifts not use them precisely as they wish? Why should I not, on the one hand, practise asceticism to show that my state is the equal of the angels; and on the other hop into bed with my stepmother to show that Christ has freed me from the moral prejudices of a bourgeois world? Does not Jesus spell freedom? Freedom has, at Corinth, become the determining mark of the church.

This manifestly presented the apostle with problems. Let us see how he set out to handle them in chapters 8–10 of 1 Corinthians. He has to bring home to them their two main mistakes, while accepting and indeed reinforcing their major premise that Christ had set them free. They failed to take with sufficient seriousness the fallenness of their human nature, and thus they gave way to misusing their freedom. What is more, they had a religion of the resurrection which did not make sufficient room for the pattern of the cross.

MISUSE OF FREEDOM

It is all too easy to see how this church, intoxicated as it was with freedom, turned Christ's liberty into licence.

'My speech is free,' they maintained. It is indeed. And yet – what of the divisions (1 Cor. 1:10–15, 3:1–9), the litigiousness (1 Cor. 6:1–8), the complaining (1 Cor. 10:10), the rudeness (2 Cor. 10:5, 12:19f.), the boasting (2 Cor. 11:16–29) to be found in their midst?

'My knowledge is liberation,' they said (1 Cor. 8:1). True again. They were liberated from the age-long fear of idols by knowing Christ, the living and true God. But they took their freedom further than that. They felt free to go and eat sacrificial celebratory suppers in an idol's temple. They cocked a snook at fuddy-duddy Christians who were traditional enough to object. But knowledge puffs up, Paul has to remind them, while love builds up – into a character like the truly free man, Jesus Christ (1 Cor. 8:1). As he sadly pointed out, it is all too easy by the exercise of our much-vaunted knowledge to injure another brother for whom Christ died (1 Cor. 8:7–13).

'My worship is free,' they might have said. No more of these dull Jewish synagogue services. None of this dead old liturgy. Let it be free! Let anyone contribute as he likes. Let anyone go on for as long as he likes. Let everyone flaunt his own gift and do his own thing without crippling regard to other peoples' wishes. First come first served at the love-feast, and hard luck on the latecomers. Ah, but that is to forget whose house you are in, whose supper you are eating, whose Body you are despising (1 Cor. 11:20–22). Such exercise of freedom forgets the impact it will have on those who come in from the cold (1 Cor. 14:23). It forgets the custom of the churches of God (1 Cor. 11:16, 14:36).

'My relationships are free,' was a war cry at Corinth. 'All things are lawful for me' (1 Cor. 6:12). Yes indeed. Our relations are wonderfully liberated in Christ, where every man is a brother and every woman a sister in Christ. And yet it is all too easy for such familiarity to sink to contempt; for such intimacy to degenerate to debauchery. Indiscipline can turn prize fighters into wrecks (1 Cor. 9:24f.). The scriptures are given for our warning and instruction. They plainly show how the Israelites, intoxicated by their free relationships, gave way to licence and idolatry and were sternly judged by God (1 Cor. 10:1–12). In any case, how about our freedom to let love control our actions and put other Christians first (1 Cor. 13:5f.)?

'My actions are free,' they said. 'I can do what I want. I find it intolerable that anyone should tell me what to do. I have my rights.' And Paul replies that they have forgotten two things. One, the church is not a democracy, still less anarchy, where everyone does what he wants. It is a Body, Christ's Body, where each limb has a particular task to do. True liberty and harmony come when we are doing what we were made for. Our freedom cannot be used in such a way as to impede the freedom of others. Moreover, the free man has to carry the responsibilities of freedom. And that is to follow the truly free man, Jesus Christ, down the path of selflessness and suffering. That is what the apostles have done, and thereby set an example (1 Cor. 4:9–16). That is what all Christians are called to do. Free though we are, we have been bought with a price, the precious lifeblood of Christ (1 Cor. 6:20, 7:23).

'My attitudes are free,' is the final plea. 'I shall please myself in what I do about special days or foods offered to idols or any other stupid taboos.' But that is a dangerous attitude. As the first part of 1 Corinthians 10 points out, it can be fighting against God. And as the second part makes plain, it can open the door for evil forces to enter and control the Lord's free man (1 Cor. 10:21–2). This they had forgotten in their lust for total freedom. They had shut their eyes to the corruption in the human heart which makes the idea of total freedom a mirage. And they had turned their back on the way of the cross.

If we are to avoid their mistakes at Corinth, we would do well to consider this basic definition. Freedom is not licence to do what I want, but liberation to do what I ought.

GUIDELINES FOR FREEDOM
Paul gives four clear guidelines for the proper use of our Christian freedom. They have a wide application. One of the glories of the Christian faith is that it does not confront us with an extensive list of commands and prohibitions, with sanctions attached. It tells us that we are Christ's freedmen, and gives us principles for ensuring that the freedom which is our spiritual birthright shall not be eroded. How we apply those principles is a matter between us and our Lord: we shall one day stand before him and give an account of how we have behaved (2 Cor. 5:10). The correlative of liberty is accountability.

Now for the guidelines given us in these letters.

First, we are free but under the law to Christ (1 Cor. 9:21). Christian churches tend either to settle for a moral indifferentism where no discipline is exerted and anything goes; or else relapse into a strongly authoritarian structure which reaches its nadir in cults like the Children of God. But Christ offers us a third way. He asks us to subordinate our freedom to the one who set us free; to seek to please him in our ethical decisions. It is a wonderfully liberating thing to be bound not to a legal code but to a person who loves us and wants our welfare above all else. It is no pain to please such a person. If we make that our aim, we shall have discovered the clearest guideline to the responsible use of freedom. Take an example from normal social life. We tend to invite to supper our friends and peers: Jesus often entertained the poor and sick. Are we going to stick to the conventions of social life or are we going to please him in a matter like this? The way of the world demands a pay rise every year for those in work, while the numbers of those out of work rocket to unprecedented heights. What would Jesus do under such circumstances? Would he not refuse a rise? This principle of seeking to please Christ is very radical!

Second, we are free whatever our circumstances. 'He who was called in the Lord as a slave is a freedman of the Lord. Likewise he who was free when called is a slave of Christ' (1 Cor. 7:22). As Christians our freedom does not depend on outward circumstances. When we feel that it does, we are allowing our freedom to be corrupted. Many courageous prisoners have shown that you can be free in a prison cell or a mental hospital, or under an alien political regime. Think of a Solzhenitsyn, a Bunyan, a Wurmbrand. I recall hearing a black South African applying Matt. 5:41, 'If any one forces you to go one mile, go with him two miles.' When forced by whites to do something he did not want, he would do it cheerfully and then ask if there was any other way in which he could be of service! That man was free, in oppressive circumstances. Jesus displayed that quality of freedom in Herod's courtroom. Freedom does not depend on circumstance, but on attitude.

Third, we are freed to be everybody's servant (1 Cor. 9:19f.). Released from the shackles of selfishness we are set free for the service of others. Of course, it does not always work out like that. We remain fallen human beings, but once a man begins to follow Christ he tries to make the good of others one of the guidelines for his exercise of freedom. This may well involve a double subordination of his own freedom.

He will be prepared to subordinate his freedom to evangelise others. Paul explained how costly this proved in his own life, and how flexible he found it necessary to become. 'For though I am free from all men, I have made myself a slave to all, that I might win the more. To the Jews I became as a Jew, in order to win Jews . . . To those outside the law I became as one outside the law – not being without law toward God but under the law of Christ – that I might win those outside the law . . . I have become all things to all men, that I might by all means save some' (1 Cor. 9:19–23). Paul did not care much about a reputation for outward consistency. He was more concerned about the inner consistency of using his freedom in the service of those who were still bound, whatever the shape of their fetters. He would not, for example, have tolerated the middle-class captivity of the church in the Western world. He would have been as active in evangelising skinheads as undergraduates. He would have been as much at home talking of Christ in the bar or the open air as at the supper party.

We are called to subordinate our freedom not only to winning people for Christ but also to helping them along the Christian road. '"All things are lawful,"' concedes the apostle, 'but not all things build up. Let no one seek his own good, but the good of his neighbour' (1 Cor. 10:23–4). Paul gives as an example meat bought in the market. Much of this meat will have been offered to some idol before sale. As Christ's freedman this does not bother him. So when he is invited out to dinner, he eats what is put before him, and asks no questions. However, if his host observes, '"This meat has been offered in sacrifice,"' then out of consideration for the man who informed you, and for conscience sake – I mean, his conscience, not yours – do not eat it' (1 Cor. 10:28–9). You have only to apply that to the use of alcohol in today's society to see how truly liberated, and liberating, a principle it is.

Fourth, as free men we must not be brought back into bondage. '"All things are lawful for me," but I will not be enslaved by anything' (1 Cor. 6:12). The man who is freed by the Lord will be a fool if he imperils his freedom by what he allows himself. We ought to ask ourselves whether our bed, our smoking, our possessions, our food, our drink are getting a grip on us which it is not easy to break. In that case, we should make the requisite changes, in the strength which Christ supplies. However permissible they may be for others, for us they are poison. They are ruining our Christian freedom. Paul applies this sharply to himself. 'Am I not free?' he asks in 1 Cor. 9:1. Free to marry or not. Free to preach the way he thinks fit. Free to accept payment or not. But he ends the chapter solemnly. 'I pommel my body and subdue it, lest after preaching to others I myself should be disqualified' (1 Cor. 9:27). He says as much to the Galatians. 'For freedom Christ has set us free; stand fast therefore, and do not submit again to a yoke of slavery' (Gal. 5:1).

We need to grasp the privileges and responsibilities of Christian freedom, and not be dominated by the pressures, inhibitions or permissiveness of the society round about us. Christian freedom is a very beautiful plant. It can flower anywhere. It blooms not for its own benefit but for others. It is always looking to the sun. And it refuses to allow bindweed to stifle it. Few flowers in the Christian garden have a sweeter scent.

CHAPTER ELEVEN

GIVING

Giving is a major subject for discussion – and evasion – in most congregations. It is a very tender issue, to be handled with great care. St Paul was no exception. He spends two whole chapters on it, 2 Corinthians 8 and 9.

In 1 Cor. 16:1 he had broached the subject of a great collection for poor Christians at Jerusalem, to be gathered from his Gentile churches. Gal. 2:10 shows that it was much on his mind at this time in his life. He had wanted the Corinthians to have their contribution ready for him to take to Jerusalem when he came. In 2 Corinthians 8 and 9 he raises the matter again. The more unimaginative of New Testament critics suspect the conflation of two separate Pauline letters in these two chapters, but then we must assume that they have not had wide exposure to church finance! Those who have will appreciate that Paul is writing to thank them for what they have already done, but also to make clear to them that it is not enough! Two chapters is not too much to secure the required balance. For giving is a powerful indicator of spiritual life. Is our giving regular? Is it free and generous? Is it proportionate to the way God has blessed us? Is it a significant proportion of our income? Is it something that is prayed over? Or do we view it as a sort of tax, a deplorable necessity, or an unmentionable subject?

In many parts of the world and the church there is no such bondage to possessions as exists in Western Christendom. In a hippie commune you will find them sharing today's good things without trying to hoard them selfishly for tomorrow. If you go to the African bush you will find a tremendous poverty combined with tremendous generosity. Good things are to be shared and celebrated when they turn up, not held on to. There is something wrong in the West with our whole attitude to money and giving. Money is like sea water. The more we have of it the thirstier we become.

But Paul had discovered that giving was exhilarating. He had himself given up home, a considerable fortune and secure prospects for the sake of the gospel, and he wanted his Corinthian friends to share in this grace too. That is why he contributes these two important chapters on the subject. I propose to examine them under four heads.

MOTIVES FOR GIVING

'The rendering of this service . . . supplies the wants of the saints,' says Paul (2 Cor. 9:12). Paul was deeply concerned about the Christian believers in the heart of a hostile Judaism in Jerusalem. They were poverty stricken, and could probably find neither work nor education. They were on the breadline, and Paul, like his Master before him, was moved with compassion. We often do not have compassion because we do not see the needs. My concern for the starving and the forty per cent unemployed in parts of Latin America was not stirred until I had seen it for myself. Then I cared, and wanted to give. It was impressive to see in Guatemala, for example, how the Christians had been conspicuous in support after the terrible earthquake. Many of the one-roomed 'temporary' housing units had been put up by Christians, and believers were living in among the homeless, and forming little cells of light and love among them. That seemed to me significant. In some of the toughest places in the world it is the Christians who are slogging it out by costly long-term involvement. Humanists will give money with great generosity, but to go on living among the poor and loving them to the uttermost requires greater resources than are available to the humanist: because love needs to be renewed, and it is the love of God himself that drives the believer to care and sacrifice and endure.

A second motive for giving is partnership in ministry (2 Cor. 9:12–14). Look at the interplay in these verses. 'The rendering of this service not only supplies the wants of the saints but also overflows in many thanksgivings to God. Under the test of this service, you will glorify God by your obedience in acknowledging the gospel of Christ, and by the generosity of your contribution for them and for all others; while they long for you and pray for you, because of the surpassing grace of God in you.' Here is a lovely 'togetherness'. The Lord gives to us and we thank him. We give to others in response, and they thank God for the kindness he has inspired in us. Thus, a round of thanksgiving to God takes place and it is created by this spirit of giving. It all sprang, of course, from that incalculable gift from God, Jesus Christ himself. It is as though we are cups that are filled from a spring: others drink from us, and they praise not the cup but the spring. Once we see that our money is not our own, but a stewardship from God: once we see that our Christian work is not our own but is part of the Master's world-wide plan; then we become willing, even enthusiastic for resources to be moved around at his direction. The Christian church is a partnership and Christ is both the owner of all the resources and the senior partner in the firm. What a motive for free and generous giving!

Paul brings before his readers a third motive for giving. It is the principle of harvest (2 Cor. 9:6–13). There is an inexorable principle built into this world, at spiritual levels as well as at natural. It is this. You reap what you sow. In a way it is tough to refuse the temptation to eat your seed corn, and then throw it away into the earth! But how worthwhile in the long run! It is hard to invest in Christians in the south of the Sudan whom you have never seen and probably never will, yet how worthwhile to be able to put resources in a place where the Spirit of God is manifestly at work. Sowing your seed corn rather than eating it could be seen as an enlightened form of self-interest. Christian giving is not. As we give, and are liberated from bondage to materialism, so the Lord is liberated to do things in and through us which he otherwise would not be able to do. The joyful hilarity of giving runs through the New Testament. It has the dying and rising characteristic of harvest about it: after all, is not dying and rising the core of the Christian life? So 'give and it shall be given to you; good measure, pressed down, shaken together, running over, will be put into your lap. For the measure you give will be the measure you get back' (Luke 6:38).

But the main reason for giving is the love of Jesus Christ. 'Thanks be to God for his inexpressible gift!' cries Paul in adoration (2 Cor. 9:15). That is why Paul gave to the limit. That is why he wanted them to give at Corinth. God's gift is the key that unlocks our selfishness. He has made me, has cared for me, was lacerated for me, and was crucified in naked dereliction for me. He gives me his pardon, his Spirit, his family, and all things richly to enjoy. What a Giver! It is no wonder if that sort of love begins to rub off on the recipients. Our giving is a pale but real response to his inexpressible gift. Mary of Bethany gave her most precious possession, that alabaster vase of ointment, to Jesus. Everyone said it was a waste. But it was not. It was a love-gift. And its fragrance has lasted down the ages. Alas, the church has not often adopted that reckless devotion, but when it has, men sit up and take notice. Many churches and cathedrals are disfigured by financial barometers outside them with the plea to 'save our ancient church'! We project the image of the ecclesiastical beggar, with Jesus nowhere to be seen. But down on the streets of Calcutta Mother Teresa and her dedicated sisters are pouring out the alabaster vase of their lives at the feet of Jesus in caring for the dying, because they are inflamed with love for him.

And everyone in the world receives a whiff of the fragrance of their responsive love to Jesus. It is by far the most powerful motive in Christian giving.

CHARACTERISTICS OF GIVING

There are four characteristics of giving which Paul underlines in this passage. The first is perhaps the most surprising. Generosity is a gift (*charis*) (2 Cor. 8:7). The word is used in popular parlance to denote charm and flair. It is used in biblical parlance to denote a spiritual gift. Many modern 'charismatics' concentrate, like the Corinthians, on tongues, healings and prophecy: these appear the really desirable *charismata*. They forget that giving is a facility given by God. It is a high-water mark of faith and vitality. For it is the very nature of God himself, imparted to the donor.

True giving is overflow (2 Cor. 8:2). It does not have to be extracted painfully from our unwilling pocketbooks. It flows out of hearts that have been warmed by the Lord's love. Try chipping ice off a glacier and you will find it a fruitless task. Allow the sun to warm that same glacier and begin to melt it, and the water will flow freely from it. So it is with Christian giving. There is no financial problem in the church: only a spiritual problem. The Lord has plenty of money lying locked up in the pockets of his people. When they are thawed by his love, it begins to flow. Look at the words Paul employs here to show how the Macedonians had given. This collection was no sort of tax: they gave 'of their own free will' . . . with 'abundance of joy' . . . 'begging us earnestly for the favour of taking part'. As Paul delightfully put it, 'God loves a cheerful [lit. hilarious] giver' (2 Cor. 8:2–4, 9:7).

Third, Christian giving must be sacrificial giving (2 Cor. 8:3). It does not matter how much it is. It does matter that it should cost us something. His giving cost him everything. Ours cannot be cheap. Macedonia was a poor province, and the Christian community there were evidently quite impoverished. Yet this is the testimony Paul gives to them and their giving: 'In a severe test of affliction, their abundance of joy and their extreme poverty have overflowed in a wealth of liberality on their part. For they gave according to their means, as I can testify, and beyond their means.' They gave when they were poor. They gave when some crisis had hit them. They gave according to their means – and how many do that? They shared the same spirit of sacrifice which was in their Master. Their giving was stamped with the character of his own.

Fourth, their giving was eminently practical. It was designed to meet the needs of Christians in appalling circumstances in Jerusalem. Certainly, it was an ecumenical gesture as well, as Gentile Christians supported Jewish believers at Jerusalem. But pre-eminently it was one part of the Body of Christ seeking to meet the physical needs of another part. Christian giving to specifically Christian needs is vital, and not practised enough. I sensed the importance of it in Bogota, Colombia, as I saw the circumstances of staggering need in which a Norwegian pastor and his doctor-wife were supported by believers far away in Norway. They did not give vaguely into some relief organisation, good though that would have been. They supported this couple from their midst who had gone out in practical ways to get their hands dirty and meet the needs.

PRINCIPLES OF GIVING

Several principles emerge from these chapters which have an application far wider than Corinth.

In the first place, as we have seen, their giving began with God's giving. There was nothing man-centred about it, nothing of which to boast. 'You know the grace of our Lord Jesus Christ, that though he was rich, yet for your sake he became poor, so that by his poverty you might become rich' (2 Cor. 8:9). That is why they gave.

Christian giving begins in response to the Love which sought us and sacrificed for us. It is not until the congregation is deeply in love with Christ that they will give sacrificially and gladly.

Second, their giving was stimulated by that of others (2 Cor. 8:2–4). We have already seen how the Macedonians, for all their affliction and deep poverty, gave prodigally. So often it is like that: those who can least afford it give most. I remember a woman being invited to a Zulu church. She went, and was conspicuous as the only white there. They welcomed her, translated for her, and made her thoroughly at home. They had a collection – to build a new Zulu church down the road. Later in the service, they had another collection – for Zulu Christian brethren who had no shoes. By this time, she had put in all the money she had with her. Imagine how staggered she was when they had a third collection 'for petrol for our white sister'. That woman came out with an entirely new perspective on Christian giving, because of what she had seen in others far less fortunate than herself.

Third, their giving to this collection came on top of regular giving (1 Cor. 16:2). Paul encouraged his congregations in Galatia and Corinth, and no doubt elsewhere, to set aside a sum weekly for Christian giving, a proportion of what they had received that week. This collection for the Jerusalem poor seems to have been additional to their regular giving. It was for people they had never seen. It was for people whose theology was suspect. It was for people who seemed to have bungled their finances by injudicious communalism. Yet they gave, gladly.

Fourth, it was a generous, freewill offering (2 Cor. 8:3–8, 12). Giving was one of the graces of Christian character like faith, love, knowledge and zeal. It was a mark of sincere belonging to the Lord. It was a badge of their love. Giving is the thermometer of love.

It is significant that no amount is laid down. In the Old Testament it was one tenth, and freewill offerings on top of that. In the New Testament we are given no fixed amount. We are told to give as God has prospered us; as our love for him dictates; as stewards of his wealth; as those who have been rescued by him from utter bankruptcy before God. The onus of decision lies with us.

Furthermore, it is our attitude which matters to God. He sees and judges the heart. We are not meant to be burdened. 'If the readiness is there, it is acceptable according to what a man has, not according to what he has not' (2 Cor. 8:12). God will see that those who are of a generous spirit do not go without. 'I do not mean that others should be eased and you burdened, but that as a matter of equality your abundance at the present time should supply their want, so that their abundance may supply your want.'

Finally, their giving all sprang from self-giving (2 Cor. 8:5). The Macedonians, of whom Paul is speaking here, did not just give gladly and generously. Their giving was more than that. It was symbolic. 'First they gave themselves to the Lord.' There is a giving that is cold and calculating. How much is expected of me? How much will others give? And there is also a giving that is warm and excitable, bubbling up from the heart. The giving of a child at Christmas to his father – giving which says, in effect, 'Daddy, I love you. This is a mark of my love.' Such giving is characteristic of churches that have caught the flavour of Christ. It is symbolic of their total surrender to him. That is what the greater Giver looks for.

RESULTS OF GIVING

Many of the results were long term and intangible, but the apostle does envisage several important by-products of Christian giving which come as a direct result of generosity.

First, needs were met; not only the needs of the Jerusalem Christians to whom they gave, but their own needs. 'And God is able to provide you with every blessing in abundance, so that you may always have enough of everything and may provide in abundance for every good work' (2 Cor. 9:8). It is remarkable but true, as many Christians will testify, that when you do give sacrificially, more than you think you can afford, God supplies your own needs.

Second, their characters were refined (2 Cor. 9:10, 13). The harvest of their righteousness was increased. It always is. Giving purges the character from the constricting grip of materialism, and allows the buds of other virtues, hidden underneath the creeper, a chance to show and grow.

Third, they met need, and evoked thanks and prayer among God's people (2 Cor. 9:12, 14). There was an overflow of thanks and praise to God for needs being met and for generosity flowering in the donors. As a result the recipients began to pray joyfully, earnestly and gratefully for those who had given. Thanksgiving and prayer were released and stimulated within the Body of Christ. And that could not fail to be beneficial.

Fourth, God was glorified. People began to notice their obedience, and acknowledge what power the gospel of Christ could have among them (2 Cor. 9:13). As a result God was 'glorified': that is to say, something of his light was reflected in their giving. True Christian giving has that effect. Believers do not boast of what has been achieved. They praise God for generous hearts and for needs met. The glory goes to him.

And finally, they became magnetised afresh by God's great gift (2 Cor. 9:15). Time and again Paul has come back, during his discussions of finance, to the cross of Christ and the supreme self-giving of the Saviour which is the model and the measure for Christian giving. Now at the end he brings it to the fore again. Thanks be to God for his inexpressible gift! And that is what all Christian donors feel. However great their sacrifice, they know it is puny in comparison with his. They know it is evoked only by the magnetism of his. And they know it is useless unless he, the supreme Giver, takes and breaks and uses their contribution in his work. Christian giving takes us to the heart of God.

CHAPTER TWELVE

SEX

Corinth was the Vanity Fair of the ancient world. Aphrodite was worshipped there as *Pornē* (prostitute), her temple on the Acrocorinth was given over to debauchery, and the very name of Corinth was used to denote fornicating ('Corinthianising'). The city was sex mad.

How did the church react? In two ways. One lot said, 'All things are lawful for me' (1 Cor. 6:12). They were permissive Christians who were indistinguishable in their sexual mores from the pagans round about them. The other lot were so revolted by all this sexual licence that they became ascetic, wanted to contract out of the whole thing, and said, 'It is well for a man not to touch a woman' (1 Cor. 7:1). Needless to say, this provided a very tricky pastoral problem. How was Paul to handle two such diverse attitudes? Chapters 6 and 7 of 1 Corinthians show us the brilliant way in which he did it. They do not give us the whole of his teaching on marriage: we must go to Ephesians 5 for that. But in these two chapters he answers specific questions which the Corinthians posed on the subject and gives them much else that they need to hear. For their age, like our own, had a warped attitude towards sexuality, singleness and marriage.

THE PERMISSIVE LIFE

Paul does not spend a great deal of time on this, but what he has to say is concentrated and well worth weighing. We can conveniently divide his teaching into heterosexual and then homosexual activity outside marriage.

Paul gives a resounding and well-thought-out 'No' to the permissive heterosexuals who argued that because Christians are not bound by food laws they are not bound by sex laws either (1 Cor. 6:13). It is not so much that promiscuity is forbidden, he tells them; it is intrinsically impossible. Why? The key lies in the word 'body'. It means a lot more in the New Testament than animal tissue. It means me. My belly will perish and turn to dust. My 'body' *sōma*, is myself. That is why the Corinthian argument drawing a close parallel between food and sexuality falls to the ground. Paul marshals no less than six arguments against sex outside marriage.

First, our body matters to God. 'The Lord [is] for the body' (1 Cor. 6:13). This staggering assertion shows that in some ways Christianity is the most earthy of faiths. If the Lord is for the body, then it matters very much what we do with it.

Second, our body will be raised. We shall have to live with it for ever. I do not think this emphasis of Paul's involves crude literalism: it is saying that the same destiny which awaited Christ's body at the resurrection awaits ours at the last day – transformation and continuity. 'God raised the Lord and will also raise us up by his power' (1 Cor. 6:14). Sex involves not just the genitals but the whole person, and therefore participates not only in the transience of the earthly life but in the continuity of the resurrection life.

Third, our body is indwelt by the Holy Spirit as his temple (1 Cor. 6:19). In chapter 3 this image is applied to the community of Christians, here to the Christian individual. Disunity wrecks the former and immorality the latter. Because the Holy Spirit indwells us, he naturally seeks our holiness.

Fourth, our body is harmed by immorality (1 Cor. 6:18). 'The immoral man sins against his own body.' There are plenty of other sins, like drunkenness, which affect the body both physically and in terms of total personality: this one emphatically does. Perhaps the Corinthians claimed, 'Every sin that a man commits is outside the body,' to which Paul replies, 'The immoral man sins against his own body.' But maybe Calvin is right, 'He does not completely deny that there are other sins, which also bring dishonour upon our bodies, but that these other sins do not leave anything like the same filthy stain on our bodies as fornication does.' It harms people deeply in their ego, and that is a good reason for avoiding it.

Fifthly, for a Christian fornication is daylight robbery. 'Shall I . . . take the members of Christ and make them members of a prostitute? Never! Do you not know that he who joins himself to a prostitute becomes one body with her? For, as it is written, "The two shall become one flesh"' (1 Cor. 6:15–16). Paul says that wrongful sexual relations constitute a rebellious act of independence, indeed robbery, from Christ (*aras* in verse 15 suggests violent wrenching away). At the same time they constitute a shameful act of dependence on a prostitute.

Sixthly, our body belongs to Christ. He died to gain possession of it. So 'You are not your own; you were bought with a price. So glorify God in your body' (1 Cor. 6:19–20). Glory to Christ, not greed for self – this is what should characterise the use of our bodies. They are not ours, but his. He died for them and possesses them. Sevenster, the expert on Seneca (a Roman contemporary of St Paul), writes, 'It is inconceivable that such a statement could come from Seneca. For him the soul, the spirit could glorify the gods, but this is impossible for the contemptible body which always threatens the purity of the soul.' Paul knows, however, that the soul is far from pure, and also that the Spirit of Christ, indwelling the body purchased by Christ, can indeed bring glory to God.

For all these reasons, says Paul, 'Shun immorality' (1

Cor. 6:18). If Christians are to take him seriously this is going to have a tremendous effect on the magazines we read, the films we see, the company we keep, the whole rigmarole of dating and petting. The body is for the Lord. We are called to keep it that way, and it is only possible through the power of the indwelling Holy Spirit.

So much for permissive heterosexuality. What about the homosexuality which has become such a major issue these days? We seem to forget that it was an even more common matter in antiquity, greatly practised and frequently discussed.

Paul does not give a full-length discussion of the subject in these letters, but he does make two basic points.

The first is that homosexuality will not pass muster for the Christian. In 1 Cor. 6:9–11 Paul writes, 'Do you not know that the unrighteous will not inherit the kingdom of God? Do not be deceived; neither the immoral [lit. those who go with prostitutes], nor idolaters, nor adulterers, nor sexual perverts [passive homosexuals *malakoi* nor male homosexuals *arsenokoitai*], nor the greedy [often used of active homosexuals], nor the drunkards, nor revilers, nor robbers will inherit the kingdom of God. And such were some of you . . .' Paul is not making a special sin out of homosexuality. He simply handles it in the same way as theft, abuse, drunkenness and fornication. He says that it is wrong, and that this is not the way to get into the kingdom of God. He goes back, like Jesus himself and like any Jew, to Genesis. There the image of God is said to reside jointly in the male and the female (Gen. 1:27), and 'Therefore a man leaves his father and his mother and cleaves to his wife, and they become one flesh' (Gen. 2:24). Sex is given either for the marriage of one man and one woman during their lifetime, or else for celibacy. This is the hard teaching of the Bible. Adultery, fornication, sodomy, polygamy, bestiality, homosexuality are all to be found in the Bible, but are all repudiated. This is not what God intended sex to be used for. All break the one-flesh unity of man and woman in which God's image is found. Accordingly, it is no surprise to find that every reference in the Bible to homosexuality is a dissuasive (see e.g. Gen. 19, Judg. 19:22f., Lev. 18:22, 20:13). There is no variation in the New Testament either in the ideal set forward of marriage or celibacy; or in the repudiation of sexual deviations form this norm (e.g. Rom. 1:24–32, 1 Tim. 1:8–10, 2 Pet. 2:6–10, Jude 7, 1 Cor. 6:9). For the Christian, active homosexual behaviour is not legitimate.

And if this seems very hard, particularly for those with a natural predisposition towards their own sex, Paul has some good news. Homosexuality can be changed. 'Such were some of you,' writes the apostle, and continues triumphantly, 'But you were washed, you were sanctified, you were justified in the name of the Lord Jesus Christ and in the Spirit of our God' (1 Cor. 6:11). That verse speaks volumes. It shows the sort of people who formed the Corinthian church. It shows the weaknesses to which they were prone, from which they had been forgiven, and which were being eradicated in them by the Holy Spirit. I have seen both male and female homosexuals come to Christ, and once their bodies have been indwelt by the Holy Spirit I have seen them either change in sexual preference so that they become oriented towards the other sex and in due course marry, or else remain single and content for Jesus' sake. It simply is not true to say that the homosexual orientation cannot be broken. It can and it is . . . once people commit themselves to Christ, welcome his transforming Spirit into their lives, and are willing for the change to come about.

THE UNMARRIED LIFE
It was not very difficult for Paul to show the licentious Christians at Corinth that theirs was not the best way. The ascetics, who in reaction against the excesses in the temple of Aphrodite turned their back on sex completely, presented a more difficult pastoral problem. The statement of 1 Cor. 7:1 sounds so Christian – but not for the reasons they adduced. There was a lot of spiritual pride and false

spirituality in their attitude. They wrongly looked on sex as disgusting. So they urged engaged couples not to go through with it; they urged Christian partners to leave their non-Christian spouses; they urged Christian couples to forego intercourse. Their view was just as warped as the licentious Christians they despised. So Paul seeks in these chapters to remove the glamorous wraps off both the single and the married state. In the olden days it was the single state that had all the glamour. Jerome and the monks took 'It is well for a man not to touch a woman' (1 Cor. 7:1) to mean 'It is best'. The unmarried state then began to be thought of as holier. These days it is marriage that has all the glamour – almost as though there was something odd or pitiable about the single. Paul takes both views head on, and contradicts them firmly. Whether you are married or single, the apostle insists, it is a matter of gift (1 Cor. 7:7), a matter of calling (1 Cor. 7:17) and a matter of wholeheartedness for Christ (1 Cor. 7:35).

In a society terrified by loneliness and bombarded by overt sexual invitations, the unmarried state could seem most unattractive. Paul does not agree. In 1 Cor. 7:7 he shows that both marriage and celibacy are a *charisma*, a gracious gift from God. Some of the greatest people in the world remained unmarried. John did. Jesus did. Paul did. And they were complete, loving people. To remain unmarried for Christ's sake does indeed involve cost: loneliness and sexual non-fulfilment. But there are three of its assets which are worth pondering.

It can be lovely (1 Cor. 7:1). It is *kalon*, literally 'beautiful' for a man not to touch a woman. A single woman like Mother Teresa is deeply attractive, despite the costliness of her sacrifice. If you are called to singleness, rejoice. Paul was unmarried (1 Cor. 7:7) and could wish for everyone to be like him, though he knew it was not everyone's gift. Jesus spoke in Matt. 19:12 of some who are willing to forego marriage for the kingdom's sake. That is a lovely thing.

It can be fulfilling (1 Cor. 7:7, 37–8, 40). Was Paul, was

Jesus unfulfilled? In no way. Nor need you be if you remain unmarried. I think of one unmarried friend, revelling in his teaching, his godchildren, his gardening, his wide pastoral concern. I think of another, a celibate bishop, whose home in the East End of London was always open to the children of the neighbourhood who flocked in. There was no hint of unfulfilment in these lives, because they had willingly embraced the call of God to celibacy.

It can be liberating (1 Cor. 7:28, 32–8). Paul gives in these verses two dimensions to the concept of liberation. He sees the single state as having far greater freedom to serve. And when you consider time, money, mobility, and availability that is manifestly true in many cases. And he considers also freedom from distraction. He wants to spare people being torn apart by loyalty to Christ and to partner which every married Christian knows. 'The married man is anxious about worldly affairs, how to please his wife . . . I say this for your own benefit . . . to secure your undivided devotion to the Lord' (1 Cor. 7:33, 35).

These are three strong advantages in the single life. They deserve to be well weighed by every unmarried person. You should not assume that marriage is necessarily the right thing for you. It may be. It may not be. God has a plan and the gracious ability to fulfil it waiting for those who seek his face and wait his time. Until we are willing to surrender to his will on this issue we shall never discover guidance.

THE MARRIED LIFE
Alongside the loveliness of celibacy is the loveliness of marriage. 'It is well for a man not to touch a woman.' True. But 'It is not good that the man should be alone' (Gen. 2:18). Neither better nor worse: *kalon*, lovely. At least, that is how God intended it in the Garden long ago: a foretaste of heaven. But often it turns into an embodiment of hell. It is when both partners are right with the God who made marriage, that the relationship becomes the lovely thing which God intended. There is profound attractiveness in a truly Christian home. Paul knew this. He had

stayed in the home of Aquila and Priscilla long enough to appreciate it. Maybe his portrait of Christian marriage in this chapter owes much to this couple the Corinthians knew so well. He makes four major points.

Christian marriage should be Christian. 'Only in the Lord' (1 Cor. 7:39) is his prescription. For marriage is the relation which illustrates the union between Christ and his people. The husband loves, protects and gives himself for his wife, just as Jesus does for his church. The wife loves, cleaves to and defers to her husband, as she would to Jesus. This is inconceivable if one partner is a Christian and the other is not. That is why the New Testament insists that a Christian should marry a Christian. 'Do not be mismated with unbelievers' (2 Cor. 6:14). That is the plain teaching to unmarried Christians. To disobey it is to flout Christ and court disaster. Of course, if you come to Christ after you are married, it is a different matter. In such cases the unbelieving partner is in some sense 'consecrated' by the believer (1 Cor. 7:14). God is at work in the situation. The Christian should pray earnestly for, and live consistently before, the partner who is not yet a follower of Jesus; 1 Cor. 7:16 should probably read, 'Wife, perhaps you will save your husband' (cf. 1 Pet. 3:1–2).

Second, Christian marriage should be exclusive (1 Cor. 7.2). There is to be no double standard of faithfulness for the husband and for the wife. Both are called to total loyalty to one another. Their sex relationship is exclusive of all others. So far from being restrictive, this confidence that they will always be true to one another gives great flexibility to the marriage, and great freedom of mixing and relationship with others of the opposite sex – for no man or woman has all the gifts of personality to satisfy their partners.

Third, Christian marriage should be binding (1 Cor. 7:10). Divorce is repugnant to God. The ideal is one man one woman for their lifetime. But Paul is a realist. He knows that divorce happens, even in Christian circles. If the Christian partner is rejected by the unbelieving partner, 'in such a case the brother or sister is not bound' (1 Cor. 7:15). Not bound to remain in the sterile relationship? Not prohibited from remarriage? Paul is not explicit. But he is clear that the ideal is for a broken marriage to become reconciled, or else for the partners to remain single (1 Cor. 7:11). It is interesting to notice Paul's sensitive handling of this issue. He quotes the words of Jesus, going back to the original purpose of marriage. He believes in lifelong partnership. However, there is no narrow legalism about him. He nowhere suggests that failure in this realm should exclude Christians from the church or the sacraments. However in these days of escalating breakdown not only of first but of second marriages, Christians have no reason to be ashamed of their conviction that marriage should be binding.

Fourth, Christian marriage should be balanced. It should be a blend of social, family, physical and spiritual sides.

The social side is important. The nuclear family can be too small and insular, and marriages are often enriched by offering hospitality to others, as Aquila and Priscilla did to Paul.

The family importance of marriage needs no emphasis: 'your children . . . are holy' (1 Cor. 7:14). But they will not turn out that way if they are given money and toys instead of love and time. If parents fail to encourage, discipline and apologise to their young, they need not be surprised if they turn out to be a disappointment; likewise if the parents are out at church meetings for several nights a week.

Again, the physical aspect of marriage is of the utmost importance (1 Cor. 7:4–5). You will not find in Paul any disgust with sex. Physical union not only expresses but deepens the unity of the partners. Paul certainly does not restrict intercourse to occasions when a child is desired. He advocates a regular and enthusiastic sex life. 'The husband should give to his wife her conjugal rights,' so the Revised Standard Version coyly translates it, 'and likewise the wife to her husband. For the wife does not rule over her own body, but the husband does; likewise the husband does not rule over his own body, but the wife does. Do not refuse one another except perhaps by agreement for a season, that you may devote yourselves to prayer; but then come together [literally 'come back to it again'] again, lest Satan tempt you through lack of self-control' (1 Cor. 7:3–5). Paul goes on strongly to condemn the ascetics who had been urging couples to forego intercourse. Such spiritualising of the marriage bond is fraught with dangers.

Finally, the spiritual side is crucial in Christian marriage. The partners need to give themselves to prayer (1 Cor. 7:5). Family worship, prayer together at night, personal prayer – these should all mark the Christian home.

In the light of the sheer difficulty of living out the Christian ideal of marriage, and the appalling effects it has on others when Christian marriages fail, celibacy should come back into careful consideration as a live alternative to marriage.

THE QUESTION OF VOCATION
How on earth are we to discern whether or not we are being called by God towards marriage? How can we tell whether celibacy or marriage is the right course for our lives? When fellow Christians are attracted deeply to some member of the opposite sex, here are some considerations which Paul offers for reflection.

First, there is the consideration of usefulness (1 Cor. 7:32–4). Could I be equally useful to the Lord if married, or would it inevitably curtail my usefulness to him? This consideration will need to be carefully weighed. The quantity of time available for Christian involvement may be reduced once we are married, but its quality may be enhanced. At all events, I have no right to marry unless I have honestly faced the question of the impact marriage will have on my Christian life and service.

Second, there is the consideration of distraction (1 Cor. 7:32, 35). If my friendship with a member of the other sex distracts me from my walk with Christ or my desire to serve him, then it is highly suspect. Often one sees an engaged couple sitting hand in hand during an evangelistic address, when both should have been among friends of their own sex, seeking to introduce them to our Lord.

Third, there is the consideration of timing (1 Cor. 7:26 –8). Paul encourages amorous youngsters to wait: not remain for ever but remain for now (1 Cor. 7:20, 24). A decision of this magnitude should never be made in a hurry. If he or she is really God's choice for me, I have no need to snatch! 'Those who marry will have worldly troubles, and I would spare you that,' says the apostle: the troubles of a wife, no home, no job, no income and two more years as a student!

Fourth, there is the consideration of self-control (1 Cor. 7:36). If you genuinely cannot control yourself sexually, it is much better to marry than burn. 'If his passions are strong, and it has to be, let him do as he wishes: let them marry – it is no sin.'

Finally, there is the consideration of perspective (1 Cor. 7:29ff.) 'The appointed time has grown very short; from now on, let those who have wives live as though they had none . . . and those who deal with the world as though they had no dealings with it. For the form of this world is passing away.' What can Paul mean?

He is asking his readers to face up to the ultimate question of all history. They – and we – live between the first and last Advent of Christ. And that consideration must influence our behaviour. There is a strong tendency for the married man to please his wife, and for the unmarried to be much more singleminded about pleasing the Lord. But the expectation of Christ's return should so attach both single and married to him, and so detach both from over-preoccupation with worldly cares, that whether single or married we are those who use this world (*chrasthai*) but do not cling tenaciously (*katachrasthai*) to it. The fashion of this world passes away, and so do our lives, whether or not the Lord returns during them. We are pilgrims on this earth, and that radically affects our attitude to marriage possessions and career. We live between the Advents. The 'time' has been decisively affected by the coming of Christ. From now on it is 'shortened' or 'furled', like a sail, waiting his touch on the rigging to blossom out to the full. If we have that perspective for the whole of our lives, we are less likely to mistake God's call to celibacy or marriage. In either state we shall make it our business to give our 'undivided devotion to the Lord' (1 Cor. 7:35).

CHAPTER THIRTEEN

SUFFERING

Ours is a very hedonistic culture. We regard happiness, ease and comfort as the highest goods in life, and we assume that they are ours by right. This is a failing which is prevalent among Christians. The feeling is that the Christian life is something like an insurance policy. We pay the premium of repentance and faith in Christ, and expect to have the hard times of life covered by the good Lord. When that does not happen, it is not uncommon to hear the complaint 'Why has this happened to *me*? I've never done anyone any harm.'

This view of pain is rather uncommon in the Bible. But then, so is the assumption that because we follow Christ we shall be exempt from the thorns and boulders of life! We were never promised that. 'When Jesus calls a man, he bids him come and die,' said Dietrich Bonhoeffer. And he ought to know . . . Christ, like great leaders down the ages, offers only toil, tears, blood, and sweat to those who set out on pilgrimage with him.

Suffering plays a big part in 1 and 2 Corinthians. Paul is so very human in these epistles. Not even in Galatians does he wear his heart more openly on his sleeve. You can feel the agony in his very soul as he exposes his sacrifice, his hardships, his passionate concern for a thankless church which sometimes repudiated him. Paul does not shrink from suffering, as if a bed of roses was his by right. He embraced the pain, and grew by it. That is how spiritual muscle is built, and endurance fashioned.

SUFFERING IS INEVITABLE
Paul had no illusions on this subject. Pain is an essential part of being human. He recognised this, and accepted it. He saw at least five facts of life which stared him in the face and spelt suffering.

First, there was the fact of opposition. 'Five times I have received at the hands of the Jews the forty lashes less one,' he writes. 'Three times I have been beaten with rods; once I was stoned.' In one fascinating passage he indicates that he fought with wild beasts in the arena in Ephesus, but that may well be figurative. At all events he was told he would suffer opposition when he came to Christ, and he certainly did (2 Cor. 11:24–5, 1 Cor. 15:32, Acts 9:16).

Second, there was the fact of following Christ. You cannot follow a crucified rabbi and expect to be treated like a king. It is bound to be a hard path to deny oneself, take up the cross and follow him. Obedience to Christ led Paul to dangerous places. 'Three times I have been shipwrecked; a night and a day I have been adrift at sea; on frequent journeys, in danger from rivers, danger from robbers, danger from my own people, danger from Gentiles, danger in the city, danger in the wilderness, danger at sea, danger from false brethren; in toil and hardship, through many a sleepless night, in hunger and thirst, often without food, in cold and exposure' (2 Cor. 11:25–7) – an astonishing list of hardships that would certainly have killed any man who was not so tough and determined. They graphically illustrate what it meant to lay down one's life for Christ in the days of the first century. In the end, inevitably, he sealed his testimony to Christ with his blood.

Third was the fact of the failures of his churches. I call them 'his' because he founded them, agonised over them, loved them like a nurse, like a father. His indignation over the failures at Corinth, his love for them, his stinging rebukes, his anger, his forgiveness, his inability to rest until he knew whether or not they would accept his strictures – all these show how seriously he took 'the daily pressure upon me of my anxiety for all the churches. Who is weak, and I am not weak? Who is made to fall, and I am not indignant?' (2 Cor. 11:28–9).

Fourth, there was the fact of frailty and weakness. Even his wiry frame gave way at times. 'Often near death' is how he shrugged it aside (2 Cor. 11:23), but what physical afflictions must lie behind that! He tells us of the illness he had which nearly made away with him in Asia. Then there was the mysterious 'thorn in the flesh' for which he sought relief and found only the Lord's strength to bear it (2 Cor. 1:8f. 12:7f.). We do not know what that ailment was, which may be as well, but we cannot doubt that it was serious. And at the time he wrote 2 Corinthians he was no longer expecting to see the return of Christ himself, but was reconciled to having to face death. He realised his body was growing weaker, and he accepted the pain which that inevitably brought with it. 'We do not lose heart,' because 'though our outer nature is wasting away, our inner nature is being renewed every day. For this slight momentary affliction is preparing for us an eternal weight of glory beyond all comparison' (2 Cor. 4:16–17).

And behind all these stood the great outside enemy, often laughed at in the modern church, but taken with deadly seriousness then and whenever the church has been most alive: the fact of Satan was bound to cause suffering. That old enemy of man was always out to mar and to spoil God's creation in any way he could. Illness was one such way. 'This woman, a daughter of Abraham whom Satan bound for eighteen years,' was how Jesus once described a sick woman, and Paul sensed the same satanic force behind his thorn in the flesh. He perceived it as 'a messenger of Satan' (Luke 13:16, 2 Cor. 12:7).

These facts, taken together, meant that suffering occasioned Paul no surprise. Nor should it surprise us.

SUFFERING IS VARIED

We have already seen that Paul had to put up with many different kinds of suffering. In 2 Corinthians 11 he outlines an astonishing catalogue: hard work, fatigue and exhaustion, imprisonment and lashes almost resulting in death, shortage of food, drink, rest, sleep and shelter. The cold and the exposure brought suffering. But far greater were the pains imposed by responsibility as he had to care for the churches at large and for factions and individuals within them. The suffering which comes from disappointment, especially from false friends, is agonising. And to see those you love being wronged or falling away from Christ brings anguish along with the indignation and the sympathy (2 Cor. 11:23–9). In chapter 4 he lets us into several other ways in which he suffered. There was the suffering of no response to the proclamation of Christ. The suffering of sacrifice to the uttermost. The suffering of overwork, as age begins to tell and weakness to bite. The suffering of what he calls 'this slight momentary affliction' (2 Cor. 4:12–17). If ever a man knew the variety of suffering it was Paul. And I hear not one word of complaint.

SUFFERING IS A PRIVILEGE

When he wrote to the Philippians, Paul said a remarkable and to us most unfashionable thing. 'It has been granted to you that for the sake of Christ you should not only believe in him but also suffer for his sake' (Phil. 1:29). Suffering was to him not a problem but a privilege. And certainly he treats it like that in his own life. 'Why,' says the commentator Strachan, 'he wears his pains like decorations.' He was warned on the Damascus road of the great things he must suffer for Christ, and he learnt to welcome them, and to glory in his weakness. 'If I must boast,' he says, when goaded beyond endurance by the smugness of the false apostles to present his own credentials, 'I will boast of the things that show my weakness' (2 Cor. 11:30). His sufferings were his greatest blessings. They taught him lessons that he would otherwise have been hard put to learn.

SUFFERING IS A TUTOR

Suffering taught him sympathy (2 Cor. 1:4). By temperament he was not a man who suffers fools gladly. But suffering so enabled him to draw on the comfort of God that he was able to comfort others when hard times hit them. That is an experience which has been multiplied down the ages. There are few afflictions that cannot be turned to good account in this way.

Suffering taught him a deep reliance on God (2 Cor. 1:9–10). This event, whatever it was, that brought him to the brink of death, had one marvellous effect. It sapped the weed of self-reliance in Paul. It taught him, in his impotence and weakness, that even he could not achieve things by trusting in himself. His only hope lay in God who raises the dead.

Suffering goes one step further. It not only casts the believer into the arms of the Lord. It gives him a deep confidence that the God who has delivered him out of that terrible predicament is well able to control and look after all the circumstances of the rest of his life. I myself had an experience a little like Paul's, when I came to the verge of death. And I can vouch for these two fruits that an experience such as that can produce. It certainly can deepen reliance on the Lord; and, if you recover, you are very confident that nothing in all the world can separate you from his love and care. It gives great confidence for the future.

There are a whole cluster of good things that came out of this occasion when Paul nearly died. He records them for us in 2 Corinthians 1. They included renewed comfort and encouragement for himself, and two visits instead of one for them. Further, the apostle's suffering led to a burst of prayer for him going up from all over the church of God, followed by a paean of praise when God answered that prayer and Paul recovered (2 Cor. 1:11). We are so prone to grow slack in prayer; suffering drives us back on the Lord, since, to our shame, we call on him with greatest earnestness when we are in trouble! No matter, he can use even the blunt instrument of suffering to encourage us to seek his face, and subsequently return to give him thanks.

Most important of all, suffering teaches us likeness to Christ. This is one of the supreme lessons which Paul has been taught by his experiences as an apostle, and which he is anxious to impart to the pleasure-hungry Corinthians. The plain fact is that suffering, willingly accepted, unites believers with their suffering Lord. As he tells the Colossians, there is a sense in which 'I rejoice in my sufferings for your sake, and in my flesh I complete what is lacking in Christ's afflictions for the sake of his body, that is, the church' (Col. 1:24). Or, as Peter puts it in 1 Pet. 4:13, 'Rejoice in so far as you share Christ's sufferings, that you may also rejoice and be glad when his glory is revealed.' Paul's own characteristic way of expressing it in the Corinthian letters is to show that suffering brings him to share the fate of his Master. 'I think that God has exhibited us apostles as last of all, like men sentenced to death; because we have become a spectacle to the world, to angels and to men . . . We hunger and thirst, we are ill-clad and buffeted and homeless, and we labour, working with our own hands . . . We have become . . . as the refuse of the world, the off-scouring of all things' (1 Cor. 4:9–13). Clearly he sees the true apostle sharing the suffering of his Lord. In 2 Cor. 4:10–12 he puts it more sharply: 'always carrying in the body the death of Jesus, so that the life of Jesus may also be manifested in our bodies. For while we live we are always being given up to death for Jesus' sake, so that the life of Jesus may be manifested in our mortal flesh. So death is at work in us, but life in you.' He has been relating some of his hardships, voluntarily undergone. At an external level these are the things that enable him to share in the dying-and-rising life of Jesus, as a true apostle should. At a deeper internal level, suffering helps him to put to death the self nature, so that the life of the Spirit within him may flourish and flow out to others. Death at work in him . . . life in those he serves.

And all this is the positive fruit of suffering, God's strange tutor.

SUFFERING IS THE PATHWAY TO POWER

We must end this survey of the place played by suffering in the life of the great apostle by looking at 2 Corinthians 12. Paul explains how, like countless sufferers since his day and before it, he earnestly asked God for the removal of this 'thorn in the flesh'. His prayer was heard, but it was not granted. Instead, God granted something better. He gave his grace to Paul so that he would have the power to bear it. 'He said to me, "My grace is sufficient for you, for my power is made perfect in weakness".' Paul does not complain. God knows what he is doing. So Paul rejoices. 'I will all the more gladly boast of my weaknesses, that the power of Christ may rest upon me. For the sake of Christ, then, I am content with weaknesses, insults, hardships, persecutions, and calamities; for when I am weak, then I am strong' (2 Cor. 12:9–10).

Paul's extremity was God's opportunity. He faced circumstances at which we usually kick (because we have not learnt the lesson of power through weakness) and he could rejoice in them. Let us look at that list outlined in 2 Cor. 12:10.

He could rejoice when he was ill. He could face 'weaknesses' with calm, knowing the Lord had a purpose in it, drawing on the presence of the Lord in the midst of it. There he found Christ's strength made perfect in weakness.

He could rejoice in 'humiliations'. None of us likes being slighted, and Paul had a fiery temperament. He had to face more humiliations and rebuffs than most men. He was constantly accused of being no apostle, of being a false apostle, of being a travelling salesman, a trickster, a weathercock. That hurt. It hurt most of all when it came from those he had himself brought to the faith. But he had learnt to take this painful thing to Christ and claim his power to bear it. And he found that Christ's power was indeed made perfect in his weakness.

He could rejoice in his 'needs'. What these are he does

not specify. No doubt they differed at different times. But the experience of need tends to take our eyes off the Lord. In this context it might have been the tendency to boast, the pain of his thorn in the flesh, or the frustration that it did not grow any better. But in turning to the Lord he found that Christ's strength was made perfect in weakness.

He could rejoice when 'subject to attack'. *Diōgmos* is a strong word. It includes insults and slander, fierce opposition by pagans, by Jews, by church members, by false brethren. They ranged no doubt from rudeness to attempted murder. What provocation to give up! But Paul handed them over to Christ, and found that his strength was made perfect in weakness.

He could even rejoice when put in 'a narrow place'. *Stenochōria* is the word he uses, and it is highly evocative. It speaks of the narrow room, of the prison cell, of the smelly ship's hold, of the garret in the roof. The narrow place – not pleasant or easy for the ablest intellect of the day, the Roman citizen who once had wealth and ease at his command. But he was following one who trod the narrow way to Calvary, and he did not baulk at being hemmed in by circumstance. He simply turned it all over to Christ, and he found that Christ's strength was made perfect in his weakness.

That was his secret. That is why he did not complain about suffering but realised it was a privilege, and a means of drawing on the risen strength of his Lord. He had come to see that only as he knew the fellowship of Christ's sufferings would he know the power of his resurrection.

Painfully and reluctantly the church down the ages has had to learn that lesson. In our own day, it was not the State Church in Germany which compromised with Hitler, but the Confessing Church that had an impact on post-war Germany. The suffering church in Uganda whose archbishop and thousands of whose members were murdered at the orders of President Amin, was purged and strengthened by that terrible ordeal, and has had a significant part to play in the reconciliation and reconstruction of the nation. Christians who suffered in the Mau Mau risings in Kenya, Christians belonging to the underground churches in Russia and China, have acquired through their sufferings a moral authority which the rest of Christendom cannot attain. As always, the blood of the martyrs is seed. As always, the way of the cross proves to be the way of new life. There is no other way in the economy of God. The church in the West will probably remain flaccid and effete until it is called upon to suffer. We ourselves are likely to learn the most significant lessons of our lives through suffering. If Jesus had to tread this path, there can hardly be another way for us. But that is something that we, like the Corinthians, are most reluctant to accept.

CHAPTER FOURTEEN

DEATH

However hard a recession bites, the undertakers are not going to go out of business. Death is the unwelcome fact at the end of the road. And one of the great tests of any philosophy, any attitude to life, is what it makes of death.

We are not sure how the Corinthians handled death. Some of them had died since Paul preached to them about Jesus and the resurrection (1 Cor. 15:6). This raised problems, as it did in Thessalonica (1 Thess. 4:13–5:1). On the whole, it would seem that the Corinthians shied away from those problems. Theirs was a religion of the resurrection, in an already realised and spiritual sense. They revelled here and now in the powers of the age to come. They were not very interested in what happened after the last enemy had struck. Life was so exciting in the Corinthian assembly that they could not become too worked up about that. In any case, they were expecting the return of Jesus Christ in power and glory, perhaps in their own lifetime. So why worry?

But some of them did worry. Otherwise why should Paul have written chapter 15 of 1 Corinthians and chapter 5 of 2 Corinthians? It is hard not to worry when your loved ones die. It is not altogether clear whether they were worried that there might not, after all, be life after death. Is that what 1 Corinthians 15 is designed to put right? More probably, the idea of bodily resurrection repelled them. They had so given rein to the physical, that the idea of being bound to it for ever was utterly repugnant.

A CHRISTIAN ATTITUDE TO DEATH
Paul had much to teach the Corinthians in this area. In the first place, death is not the end; it does usher in a further life, as the resurrection of Jesus Christ has made abundantly plain. Therefore it is sheer folly not to give it due consideration.

But equally, death was not a friend, as Socrates had managed to persuade himself it was. It was an enemy: the last enemy (1 Cor. 15:26). And therefore it will need to be approached with awe and misgiving. Do not believe those who tell you they are not afraid of their own dissolution: they are deceiving nobody but themselves.

There was an element of dread in Paul's own approach to death. He puts it in delightful imagery in 2 Cor. 5. He says in effect, 'It is not the dress of immortality I am shrinking from. What I don't want is to be stripped naked of the clothes of this life before putting the new clothes on.' That dread must remain in every Christian heart: the dread of exchanging the known for the unknown, the now for the then.

But having said that, Paul approached death with remarkable equanimity and confidence, even with enthusiasm. In his letter to the Philippians he can write 'To me to live is Christ, and to die is gain . . . My desire is to depart and be with Christ, for that is far better. But to remain in the flesh is more necessary on your account' (Phil. 1:21, 23–4). Even after staring death in the face, he can speak about it calmly. 'We were so utterly, unbearably crushed that we despaired of life itself. Why, we felt that we had received the sentence of death; but that was to make us rely not on ourselves but on God who raises the dead; he delivered us from so deadly a peril, and he will deliver us; on him we have set our hope that he will deliver us again' (2

Cor. 1:8–10). He could have this peace about it because the awesome sting of death had been drawn. This was human sin, human alienation from a holy God, which would be finalised by death. Paul was well aware of that sinfulness even in his outwardly so respectable life. He knew he could not face God on his own merits. But he knew that Christ had died for him on the cross, and that as a result his sins, which were many, had all been dealt with. Accordingly, he could face death confident in the final verdict, which was due to Christ and him alone.

This was Paul's basic reason for confidence in the face of death. It made a great deal of difference. He was able to labour abundantly for his Lord, knowing that his labour was not in vain (1 Cor. 15:58). He was able to live an unselfish life for the one who for him had died and risen again (2 Cor. 5:15). He was able to cease fretting about those who had died, knowing that they were with Christ (1 Thess. 4:14). He was serene in the assurance that nothing in life or death could separate him from the love of God in Christ Jesus (Rom. 8:39). It meant he could even face the deterioration of his own bodily powers and the prospect of his own dissolution, confident in the Spirit within who renewed him daily and the prospect of having a house to live in with God once the tent of this life's abode was struck (2 Cor. 5:1). Paul could live to the full, because he was not afraid to die.

THE GROUND OF CHRISTIAN CONFIDENCE
Christians do not face death with confidence because they are blind to its horrors, or because they have not stopped to think about its implications. Their confidence rests not on supposed messages from the dead through a seance, or philosophical investigations into the survival capacity of the human ego. Extra-sensory perception has nothing to do with it, nor has the experience of those who were technically dead for a short time and revived. Christians do not pin their faith on the investigations of the Society for Psychical Research. They look unambiguously to the resur-

rection of Jesus of Nazareth after his crucifixion under Pontius Pilate.

Of course this strikes many people as naïve. He could not have risen from the grave; after all, dead men don't rise. But nobody is claiming that they do. We are claiming that *this man* rose. The man who is the ideal for all men. The man whose birth is as mysterious as his end. The man who claimed to reveal God to men, to forgive sins, to be the light of the world, to live a sinless life, to judge men at the last day, and to accept the worship of his followers. Not just any man, but this man! The resurrection of Jesus Christ is unique. It stands or falls on hard facts. What are they?

THE FACTS OF HISTORY

In 1 Corinthians 15 we have the earliest and fullest writing about the resurrection of Jesus Christ that has come down to us. It offers no less than six factors for our consideration.

First, the man who wrote it. This was Saul of Tarsus, the chief enemy of the Christian 'heresy'. He was turned round in mid-course by the resurrection (1 Cor. 15:3–4). On the Damascus road he was, as he puts it in Philippians, 'apprehended by Christ Jesus'. 'Have I not seen Jesus our Lord?' he asks in 1 Cor. 9:1 (cf. 1 Cor. 15:8). No single event apart from the resurrection of Jesus Christ has been so determinative of the course of Christian history as the conversion of St Paul. As Lyttleton put it in the mid-eighteenth century, 'The conversion and apostleship of St Paul alone, duly considered, was of itself a demonstration sufficient to prove Christianity to be a divine revelation' (*Observations on the Conversion and Apostleship of St Paul*, 1747).

Second, consider the prominence of this message. Paul delivered to the Corinthians 'as of first importance' this message of the resurrection which he himself had received with such power and joy into his life. It was the heart of Christianity. At Athens he could be satirised as proclaiming a couple of new deities to add to the pantheon, Jesus and Anastasis (i.e. 'Resurrection', Acts 17:18), so prominent in his preaching were the person of Jesus and the fact of his resurrection. The resurrection is no tailpiece to Christian doctrine. It is the centrepiece.

Third, notice the age of the tradition. Jesus was executed in A.D. 30, 31 or 33. 1 Corinthians was written in A.D. 54, some twenty years later. It would be very good tradition if the evidence went back only that far. But it goes back a lot further. Paul says, 'I delivered to you . . . what I also received.' That is to say, he passed on the message he had himself received. This immediately takes it back to within three or four years of the resurrection, when Paul was converted. The approximate date of this can be determined from Gal. 1:18, 2:1. If the 'fourteen years' of Gal. 2:1 means fourteen years after his conversion then it will have been in A.D. 35 that he came face to face with the risen Christ. If the three years of Gal. 1:18 are to be added to those fourteen years, then we must assume that he came to faith in A.D. 33, for the visit to Jerusalem can be fixed at A.D. 49. In either case, the time gap between the event and Paul's discovery of it was tiny. But even more significant than this small time gap is Paul's choice of words for 'receive' and 'deliver'. They are technical words, both in Greek and in the underlying Hebrew, for receiving and handing on authorised tradition. The resurrection fact and story were already authorised tradition in Christian circles before the conversion of St Paul! No wonder Meyer has called these verses 'the oldest document of the Christian church'.

Fourth, consider the source of this tradition. It is stressed in 1 Cor. 15:11 that Paul proclaimed precisely the same message of the resurrection as did the Jerusalem church. His message comes from the very centre of the events themselves, and within only two or three years of those events. Could one have better evidence of any historical event than this? Incidentally, two names of great significance are mentioned here, Peter and James. Both met with Jesus after the resurrection. Paul went up to Jerusalem, three years after his conversion, to question them

(Gal. 1:18). The interview of Jesus with Peter is attested, though its contents are not disclosed, in Luke 24:34, 'The Lord is risen indeed, and has appeared to Simon!' Peter calls himself 'a witness of the sufferings of Christ as well as a partaker in the glory that is to be revealed' (1 Pet. 5:1). The appearance to James is nowhere recorded in the New Testament, but in the apocryphal *Gospel according to the Hebrews* Jesus comes to James and says, 'My brother, eat your bread, for the Son of man has risen from those who sleep.' Something of the sort must have happened, for James, who was not a believer during the lifetime of Jesus, became head of the Jerusalem church after the resurrection. 'He appeared to James' (1 Cor. 15:7).

Fifth, there is a confident note of conviction in this passage which it would have been hard to fabricate. The short, staccato sentences throb with discovery and assurance. They also display a remarkable change of tense. In Greek the aorist tense is commonly used for events in the past, but the perfect for past events which have present overtones and effects. Paul writes a string of aorists: 'Christ died . . . he was buried . . . he was seen'. But when he comes to the resurrection, a mere aorist will not suffice for him. He bursts out into the perfect, *egēgertai*. It means, 'He rose, and he is alive!'

Sixth, glance at the evidence adduced. First, the historic facts. The repeated *hoti* in the Greek of 1 Cor. 15:3f. suggests to scholars that Paul is quoting a very old document, indicating 'that' Christ died according to the scriptures (such as Isaiah 53), 'that' he was buried (hint of the empty tomb), 'that' he was raised again on the third day as scripture predicted (e.g. Ps. 16:10, 53:10, 11), and 'that' he appeared to Cephas and the others. Second, Paul adduces the evidence of the resurrection appearances: Peter, the twelve, James, the 500, all the apostles, and finally himself. Third, he hints, perhaps, at what is explicit elsewhere: the changed lives which resulted from that resurrection. Peter changed from coward to martyr. The twelve changed from a rabble into a church. James changed from sceptic to

Christian leader. Paul changed from persecutor to apostle. The Corinthians changed from homosexuals, robbers and fornicators into the people of God. Remarkable evidence not only that he rose but that he lives. And all down history it has been repeated continuously, through the transformation of sinners into disciples.

The final piece of evidence which wells up from this account is the new movement itself. Christianity started. Something must have triggered it off. It had little to differentiate it from Judaism except the triumphant, exultant conviction that the long-awaited Messiah had come, had died for the sins of the world and was alive again to become potentially the companion of all.

Such were the facts from history on which Paul based his own confidence in the resurrection, and commended it to Corinth . . . and to us.

IS THE RESURRECTION OF CRITICAL IMPORTANCE?

Many people doubt it. Many want a Christianity without it. Many Christians would like to dilute it into a vague spiritual survival. Does it really matter?

Paul faces the implications if the resurrection of Jesus is false with shattering realism. If dead men never rise, then Christ did not rise. If Christ did not rise the apostolic proclamation is empty. If that is the case, then the Corinthians' faith is vain. If Christ did not rise, the apostles have misrepresented God. Believers are still in their sins, for they cannot be sure, without the resurrection, that Christ's atoning death did in fact suffice. What is more, dead Christians are not 'sleeping' but perished. Christians are of all men the most to be pitied because they are deluded about the ultimate end of man (1 Cor. 15:13–19). That is what follows if Jesus Christ did not rise from the dead.

But what are the implications if he did rise? Here are no less than ten consequences which he mentions in 1 Corinthians 15.

1. The resurrection validates the uniqueness of Jesus (1

Cor. 15:4). If he rose from the dead, that substantiates his claims (Rom. 1:3, 4). He is unlike any other teacher there has ever been.

2. The resurrection attests the achievement of Jesus on Calvary (1 Cor. 15:3). If he rose, we can be confident that his death has atoned, and that God has vindicated him. He 'was put to death for our trespasses and raised for our justification' (Rom. 4:25).

3. The resurrection initiated the gospel of Jesus (1 Cor. 15:3–11). Without it there would have been no gospel to proclaim. The Easter faith is based on the Easter event. It goes back to eyewitnesses.

4. The resurrection means that Jesus can be known today (1 Cor. 15:20). If he not only rose but is alive, then he is available, and can be met.

5. The resurrection of Jesus is the first fruits of a great crop to come. His deed has undone Adam's fall (1 Cor. 15:20–2). His resurrection points to our future if we are in him.

6. The resurrection of Jesus has robbed the last enemy of its fangs (1 Cor. 15:55–6). The unpleasantness of dying remains. The fear of what lies beyond death's wall is gone. Christ partook of our nature 'that through death he might destroy him who has the power of death, that is, the devil, and deliver all those who through fear of death were subject to lifelong bondage' (Heb. 2:14–15).

7. The resurrection of Jesus gives victory to human beings who trust him (1 Cor. 15:56–7). He can and does change our human nature, refining it and giving us a power over evil inclination which we never knew without him. As Paul puts it in Eph. 1:19–23, the power which raised Christ from the dead is available to set us free from the grip of evil.

8. The resurrection of Jesus is the pledge and model of our resurrection body on the last day (1 Cor. 15:35–8, 42–3, 49). There will be continuity of life but difference in the way that life is expressed. We shall be recognisable but glorified, like the ear of full wheat, in contrast to the grain of bare corn, before it died and rose again.

9. The resurrection of Jesus is the guarantee of his return (1 Cor. 15:51, cf. Acts 17:31). The fact that he died and rose in the past is a pledge that he will come again at the end of time, as he said he would, to bring all history to a climax.

10. And in the meantime, the resurrection of Jesus is the spur for Christian action, in the quest for justice, in service to mankind, and in the proclamation of the gospel (1 Cor. 15:57f.).

All of these consequences, negative and positive, hang on whether or not Jesus did leave the cold tomb that first Easter Day. Nobody can say it is a matter of indifference.

THROUGH A GLASS, DARKLY

There are many questions we should love to ask, and to which the answers are, at best, opaque. Here are three:

1. *Does the bodily resurrection of Jesus matter?* Why should it not have been a spiritual survival? Yes, it matters a good deal. In the first place Jews could never have conceived of a resurrection which was not in some way physical. And it is not difficult to sympathise with them. What sort of spiritual continuity is possible if Jesus' body lies mouldering in the grave? In what sense could it be *Jesus* that survives? How could they have known it to be him? Of course, resurrection is no crude resuscitation. Rabbis used to argue about whether resurrected bodies would have warts and all, or be cleaned up! That is a long cry from the resurrection of Jesus. Lazarus was resuscitated, but Lazarus had to die again. Jesus was raised to a new dimension of life. 'Christ, being raised from the dead will never die again; death no longer has dominion over him' (Rom. 6:9). There is always in the New Testament record an element of ambivalence: the disciples recognised him but they doubted, or they did not fully recognise him, and then, suddenly, they did. That speaks well for the veracity of the witnesses. They were being faced with something unheard of in the history of the world, and they were doing their best to explain it. But certainly they were trying to say that the resurrection meant the transformation of the body of Jesus

136

into a new genre, like the transposition of petrol into energy, or a sperm and ovum into a child. This continuity matters. Not only so that we may be confident of the identity of Jesus, but that we may be confident of the destiny of the world. Much that passes for Christianity these days is a form of Gnosticism where the physical does not matter in the long run. A spiritual resurrection might suffice for Christ and for his followers. But the biblical hope is not of a spiritual escape from this world; rather, of a new heaven and a new earth. God will not scrap us, but re-fashion us. The doctrine of bodily resurrection in some form or other seems essential if God's promises in and for this world are to be made good. It is not a matter of indifference that the Jesus who took our flesh and died in it; that he rose in it on Easter Day and is even now at the right hand of God as the man Christ Jesus.

2. *Is there an intermediate state?* This is another question which is often asked. The answer is, surely, yes. The constant teaching of the New Testament and not least 1 Cor. 15:49–53, is that the resurrection body will not be for any believers until it is for all. At present, only Jesus has a resurrection *body*; that is, a mode of personal expression that is final and fitting. Other believers await that, either in a state of nakedness, if you take one line of imagery (2 Cor. 5:3) or else in a state of suspended animation akin to sleep, if you take another (1 Thess. 4:16). On any showing the believer is envisaged as being with Christ, which can be described as 'gain'and as 'far better'; 'blessed are the dead who die in the Lord . . . that they may rest from their labours' (Phil. 1:23, Rev. 14:13). If you look at it from our point of view, the departed are still caught in the nexus of time and space: their souls cry out 'Lord, how long?' (Rev. 6:9f.). But seen from God's point of view (and perhaps from their own?) they 'sleep' until the last day at the return of Jesus Christ, when the dead will be raised and given their resurrection bodies, and the living will be changed into that final state without having to undergo death (1 Cor. 15:51f., 2 Cor. 5:4f.). And then we will for ever be with the Lord (1

Thess. 4:17). What will that be like? Let the author of Revelation paint the picture. 'Behold, the dwelling of God is with men. He will dwell with them, and they shall be his people, and God himself will be with them; he will wipe away every tear from their eyes, and death shall be no more, neither shall there be mourning nor crying nor pain any more, for the former things have passed away. And he who sat upon the throne said, "Behold, I make all things new"' (Rev. 21:3–5).

3. *How can we conceive of the resurrection body?* We have little to go on. But in 1 Corinthians 15 there are two pointers which go a long way. Paul's teaching that there is a wide variety of 'bodies' (i.e. forms in which the self can be expressed) in the universe is helpful. It liberates us from undue literalism about the subject, while forbidding us to take refuge in a purely spiritual survival. God will give us a means of expression for ourselves in heaven which totally befits our environment.

His other contribution comes in answer to the question, 'How are the dead raised? With what kind of body do they come?' (1 Cor. 15:35). He offers two specific, though partial, answers.

The first is that they will be like Christ's risen body: he is the first fruits of the crop, which will in due course ripen and share his nature (1 Cor. 15:23). His resurrection body was recognisably his own, yet no longer subject to the confines of time and space. It could vanish: it could also eat fish. The second partial answer comes from the grain of wheat (1 Cor. 15:37). If you had never seen an ear of corn waving in the wind of a summer's day, you would hardly believe that it sprang from that little shrivelled grain you held in your hand last winter. But there is a continuity of life which somehow survives the 'death' of that grain of corn in the ground. First the blade, then the ear, then the ripe corn in that ear, spring from the single grain. There is continuity of life, but the ear is much more glorious than the single grain. There is continuity of life, but that life is embodied in a different way. So it will be with the resurrection of the dead. 'What is sown is perishable, what is raised is imperishable. It is sown in dishonour, it is raised in glory. It is sown in weakness, it is raised in power. It is sown a physical body, it is raised a spiritual body' (1 Cor. 15:42–4).

And that, no less, is the destiny which awaits erstwhile robbers, drunkards and libertines at Corinth. That, in the infinite mercy of God, is what awaits you and me. What a difference that hope can make to the way we live, and to the way we approach bereavement and our own death. Whether the parousia intervenes, or whether we have to go through death first, our destiny is to be with him, and to be made like him, for ever.

Part Three

Problems of Authority

CHAPTER FIFTEEN

LEADERS

Leadership is vital to a church, if only because a congregation rarely rises beyond the level of its leaders. And the leaders at Corinth created a lot of problems. This can unfortunately still happen. On the whole, modern patterns of leadership leave something to be desired. Often there is little vision, little actual leadership at all; instead, an abrogation of responsibility. Sometimes there is an attempt to exercise the old monarchical pattern, as the priest (or non-episcopal equivalent) seeks to impose his will on the congregation. Sometimes division is the order of the day, as rival factions in the church put up their own candidates for office. And sometimes the magic word 'democracy' is uttered, committees proliferate, and little is done. What has the Corinthian correspondence to say about this important matter?

It certainly knows all about the difficulties. The emergence of warring factions each advocating their own candidates for leadership was the problem which actually caused Paul to write 1 Corinthians (1 Cor. 1:10f.). False leaders crept into this church and corrupted many. Timothy, and Paul himself, were violently snubbed, and probably physically manhandled. They had seen it all.

MODELS FOR LEADERSHIP

Paul does not advocate, or embody, any single model of leadership. He gives instead a number of illustrations of ways in which a Christian leader will seek to operate.

1. The nanny (1 Cor. 3:2). Paul had seen the wet nurse looking after an orphaned baby, and saving it from death by milk from her own body. That is the sort of thing he had to do in the early days of the Corinthian church among the new disciples. Any good leader needs to be able to provide basic nourishment for new Christians without giving them indigestion.

2. The father (1 Cor. 4:15). Paul seems to have two particular ideas in his mind in this image. First, he is insisting that Christian leaders need to know how to bring men and women to new birth in Christ. Second, they must be able to offer a father's guidance and discipline for young Christians – a crucial aspect of leadership in a permissive and non-directive age.

3. The example (1 Cor. 4:6f.). Leaders must give an example. If their lives are not an inducement to discipleship, their words will fall on deaf ears.

4. The clown (1 Cor. 4:10). Paul is willing to be reviled, mocked, stoned and imprisoned for the sake of Christ. He is prepared to be thought unintelligent and an object of fun and ribaldry because of his commitment to an obvious failure, a crucified Messiah. It is apposite to reflect on the role of the clown in Shakespeare – the fool who in reality is the wise man, the blind person who alone can see. Paul is willing to adopt – and advocate – that role in Christian leadership.

5. The worker (1 Cor. 3:8–9). Christian leadership involves long hours of hard work. It calls for the constant capacity to be disappointed, and to keep going. It demands persistence, a willingness to cooperate with other workers, and partnership with God.

6. The farmer (1 Cor. 3:6). Whether the role be that of sowing seed or of watering it, Christian leaders are primarily involved in the market gardening business, not in the

preservation of ancient buildings.

7. The master builder (1 Cor. 3:10). Paul sees himself as a senior Christian worker, raising a spiritual temple. He begins with laying the foundation of Christ in each life that will accept it, and then, in partnership with other leaders, seeks to build on that foundation a superstructure which is congruous with the base, and will withstand the fire of assessment on the day of judgment. He knows that if he builds selfishly he will rue the day. He knows that if he builds carelessly, he could destroy that temple by schism or by heinous sin within the members. The task entrusted to him as a wise master builder was to see a corporate temple for God being erected in the midst of carnal Corinth.

8. The servant (1 Cor. 3:5). As if that was not revolutionary enough for a Christian leader, Paul goes further and sees himself as a slave (1 Cor. 7:22, 2 Cor. 4:5). In the ancient world slavery was exceedingly common. One might have a kindly master or a perfect brute; but in either case one had no rights, no liberty to marry, no money, no assured prospect of liberation. A slave was a chattel, not a person. It is astonishing that the New Testament leaders time and again chose this word of terrible opprobrium to describe their estimate of their relation to their Lord. It expressed the total devotion they felt for him, and the complete obedience they were prepared to offer to his people. That quality of total commitment proves extraordinarily attractive.

9. The steward (1 Cor. 4:1–2). In an ancient household there was often an *oikonomos*, himself a slave, who was given responsibility over the whole household by his master. He would receive daily instructions from his employer and then see that they were carried out. All his master's resources would be available to him, but he would be accountable for the way he used them within the household. Such is the task of the Christian leader.

10. The man in the dock (1 Cor. 4:3). Paul is not too worried about what others think of him or say about him. He is not very concerned with his own self-assessment. He

is much more interested in how the Lord will estimate his work at the end of his life. And it is with that goal in mind that he lives and works in leadership and service for the Corinthian Christians.

11. The scrapings from the saucepan (1 Cor. 4:13). Paul deliberately chooses this astounding simile to describe the ultimate in filth and degradation. He wants to show them that he is willing to endure anything for Christ, and was in fact facing daily mockery and hardship as a result of his work.

12. The delegate (1 Cor. 4:19f.). The leader brings with him a savour of the powerful kingdom of God. He is its authoritative representative. Elsewhere Paul crystallises this image further, as we noted in chapter two, on Mission. He is the ambassador of Christ, albeit in chains (2 Cor. 5:20, Eph. 6:20). The ambassador speaks for his country. He represents his country's policies in an alien land. His country is judged on the basis of his own speech and behaviour. It is a most challenging model for any Christian leader.

Those dozen images come within the first few chapters of 1 Corinthians. They show the variety and complexity of Paul's understanding of Christian leadership; and they are far from exhaustive. But they show that if we entertain any monochrome conception of what it means to be Christian leaders we are certainly wrong. It is a many-splendoured thing, and it is all derived from Jesus, the leader of men who was the servant of all.

DANGERS IN LEADERSHIP
The opening of 1 Corinthians, indeed the whole of both letters, provides eloquent illustration of the dangers of leadership. Here are some of them.

1. The danger of going it alone (1 Cor. 3:5–6). Clearly some of the Corinthians had been seeing Paul, Apollos, Peter and others as independent operators, each doing his own thing. Paul insists that insofar as they are truly pastors,

they are cooperating to do God's thing. The plurality and the cooperation of pastors is strongly stressed; and it needs to be in the modern church, where Christian leaders are normally in sole charge and are often highly individualistic.

2. The danger of causing division (1 Cor. 1:12f.). There is no suggestion that Paul, Cephas, Apollos and others were setting out to create parties for themselves in Corinth, though this may possibly have been the case. Probably the camp followers were using the names of Christian leaders as ways of expressing their own need for significance . . . like football fans. This is a deeply-rooted human character-istic, and all Christians who have positions of leadership need to watch against becoming a sort of cult figure to their followers – however few. It is bad for the man, disastrous for the Christian body, and dishonouring to Christ.

3. The danger of pride (2 Cor. 12:11, 11:16–21, 1 Cor. 3:5). Clearly there were at Corinth leaders boasting of their spiritual pedigree and achievements. Paul cuts at the root of this. Any achievement we have, any quality we possess, is a gift from God: we do not boast of our Christmas presents – we are thankful for them. The same attitude should mark our Christian self-assessment (1 Cor. 4:7). So he does not even speak of Apollos and himself as people but as instruments: '*What* then is Apollos?'! Pride is one of the fastest ways of losing spiritual effectiveness, and it becomes an occupational hazard to Christian leaders.

4. The danger of discouragement (2 Cor. 4:1, 15–16). There was much at Corinth to cause Paul distress, even despair. But on the whole he did not lose heart. He had obtained mercy from God, and that drove him on. He had received from God the ministry of serving them, and that was a privilege that sustained him through hardships and disappointments.

5. The danger of deception (2 Cor. 11:13). Paul was faced by apparent colleagues who were nothing of the sort. He had the perception to see through their talk and to recog-nise them for what they were, deceitful workers, disguising themselves as emissaries of Christ. Christian charity among

leaders does not dispense with clear thinking and shrewd assessment.

6. The danger of pursuing acceptable words (1 Cor. 2:4, 1:20f., 4:19f.). Leadership involves talk. And talk can easily become an end in itself, not a stimulus to action. It is easier to preach than to practise . . . Paul has to remind his readers that the kingdom of God does not consist in talk but in power: the power of God to build a church out of the street riff-raff of Corinth, the power of God to change and transform character. That, not talk, is what it is all about.

7. The danger of pursuing spiritual kicks (1 Cor. 12–14). There is no evidence that the leaders at Corinth were more guilty of this failing than the rest of the congregation, but there was an undeniable tendency, which Paul is at pains to counteract, to judge spirituality by gifts, and to rate people in terms of their gifts (tongues, prophecy and the like) rather than their character. This led to a church which sought gifts rather than the Giver: a highly dangerous (and contemporary) failing.

8. The danger of wanting to be well spoken of (1 Cor. 4:1f.). In this passage Paul makes it plain that he does not mind what the Corinthians think of him now. He is concerned with what Christ will think of him at the Judgment. The Lord, not the Corinthians, will judge: then and not now will be the occasion. Paul refuses to be deflected from what is right by considerations of popularity. The wise leader will follow his example.

9. The danger of wanting crowns without thorns (1 Cor. 4:8). The Corinthians were 'already full, already rich, already embarked on their reign with Christ', were they? This was very dangerous. And sensible Christian leaders will warn against any theology of resurrection power which does not embrace in equal measure the way of the cross.

Those who speak of possessing 'the fulness' tend, in the first place, to become arrogant: the divide between the 'haves' and the 'have-nots' of spiritual blessings becomes more and more absolute – and the 'haves' become more and more unteachable.

Second, such a theology has a large fall-out rate. When the facts of life militate against the theory, when the heat comes on, then shallow plants wither and fade.

Third, it tends to make people gnostic. The Gnostics claimed the fulness of God's blessings *now*, and were not prepared to wait for any of them until *then*. Their realised eschatology was out of balance with the teaching of Jesus which clearly assigned fulness and perfection to a future after death.

Finally, a theology of the resurrection makes a disciple very unlike his Master. Jesus endured the cross. He taught that there were no crowns to be had without thorns. There is no path to glory save through the vale of tears, and with a crucified companion. The cross was the corrective for false ideas of leadership current at Corinth. It still is today, in our hedonistic society, eager for thrills, wanting instant results, standing on status, eaten up with self-esteem, and exceedingly reluctant to suffer. The cross exposes wrong ideals of leadership and also shows how they can be transcended.

QUALITIES IN LEADERSHIP

These letters abound in examples of the qualities needed for effective leadership, but I shall confine myself to a few from the very beginning of 1 Corinthians. They are not the qualities which most Selection Boards for ministerial candidates always go for.

First, I notice the context of prayer emerging from the very first verses of the Epistle. I notice the variety of his modes of prayer, his thanks to God for the Corinthians, his deep faith, his overflowing confidence. This leader was, above all, a man of prayer.

Next, Paul was a man who made good use of appeal (1 Cor. 1:10). He was not afraid to make strong appeal and challenge on the grounds of deep personal relations with many of his readers. Equally, he was not afraid to rebuke them thoroughly when they deserved it (1 Cor. 3:1f., 11:22). Few ministers do either.

Paul was at pains to play down personality (1 Cor. 1:12f., 3:5). Personality can be the foe of spirituality, and if people put too much faith in any one leader or type of leader they tend to fade away when he leaves and to be incapable of receiving ministry from others.

Paul was an enthusiast. And enthusiasts tend to exaggerate! It is all the more impressive, therefore, to find him extolling the value of accuracy (1 Cor. 1:16). A leader has only to be found exaggerating a few times to lose all credibility.

Another most interesting feature in Paul's leadership was his discovery and fulfilment of his role (1 Cor. 1:17). No man can do everything. The attempt to be the omnicompetent vicar is bound for failure. I do not think that Paul is denigrating the significance of baptism in this passage: that would be inconsistent with his whole theology. He is merely asserting that baptising people was not his particular sphere of ministry. He was an evangelist. Within all Christian ministry there is a crying need for men to find their own particular niche, stick to it, and release other people for contributing their gifts to the Body of Christ.

Paul was a very headstrong character, and it is all the more impressive, therefore, to find him stressing the importance of small people. How like God to choose the foolish things in the world to shame the wise, what is low and despised in the world (even the things that are not) to bring to nothing the things that are highly esteemed. Just like God – but it is not every top rabbi from the University of Tarsus who would recognise the fact. Little people matter to God, and they should matter to a good leader. It is when people know they matter that they can grow and find their potential. And the sooner the leader discovers that spiritual leadership is a quite different thing from natural leadership, the better. One hears people saying, 'Of course, there is just not the leadership potential in my inner city parish!' Really? Is that not importing the standards of the world into the gospel? Is that not doubting the God who calls into being the things that are not? I believe firmly that God gives all the necessary resources of leadership to every local church – if only they are prepared to recognise, learn from and train the right people.

That is what makes the gift of discernment so crucial for the leader (1 Cor. 2:15). We need the ability to see as God sees, and that gift is one of the most important in any leader.

Paul is clear on another very significant thing: the essence of effective speaking. It is not eloquence and preparation, important though those can be. It is testimony to God, and that testimony centres in Jesus Christ and him crucified (1 Cor. 2:2f.). Is that characteristic of most modern clergy? Do they come among their congregations with humility on the one hand, and demonstrating the power of God's Holy Spirit on the other? When that happens the church grows, for men put their faith not in the leaders, but in the power of God.

And when they have done this, and come to faith in Christ, they need teaching. Paul uses the images of the bottle and the meat (1 Cor. 3:1, 2:6). People need spiritual food appropriately broken up. Spiritual age is nothing to do with natural age or mental achievements. New babes in Christ need the bottle. They then need to be built up to take strong meat, so that they are not spoon fed, but begin to discern the mind of Christ and think and act like him. It is to that measure of independence and maturity that Christian leaders need to bring those committed to their charge. There is no higher calling than this in all the world.

CHAPTER SIXTEEN

WOMEN

St Paul has only to be mentioned in some circles to evoke the cry of 'misogynist'. Was he? The question of the place of women in the Christian community, its life and leadership, is an extremely hot contemporary issue, and as it is dealt with to some extent in the Corinthian correspondence it is well worth trying to understand St Paul on the matter.

THE BACKGROUND
Women were not highly prized in either Hebrew or Graeco-Roman culture. In the latter days of the Republic there was certainly a move towards female emancipation, but this was not encouraged by Augustus. A woman was under the authority of either her father or her husband. She could not testify in a court of law; she could not inherit property; she could not claim the right to education. Many women, particularly of the upper classes, broke out of this mould, and the satirists like Juvenal, towards the end of the first century, are full of their amorous goings on. Society was either shocked, or professed itself to be. Apart from the docile women under the authority of their menfolk, and the loose women on the rampage, there were a few highly influential courtesans who held court among the social élite.

In the Hebrew world it was not much different. Women had no rights, no education. They sat in a gallery in the synagogue. They could not share in its leadership as elders. If anything the woman's place had declined as rabbinic influence grew. In earlier days of Israel's history woman, taken from man's side to be his helpmeet, had been greatly revered in the home (Exod. 20:12, Lev. 19:3, Deut. 21:18f.), and some Old Testament women had been mighty leaders like Miriam, Deborah and Huldah. By the time of Jesus, women took no part in public life, were so heavily veiled that a man could not recognise his own mother, and were thoroughly downtrodden. 'It is better to burn the Torah than to teach it to women,' said the rabbis, and many Jewish men gave thanks to God daily, 'Blessed be God who has not made me a heathen, a slave or a woman.'

The old religion of Rome was in decay, and by the first century was being replaced by many cults from the East, most of which gave a prominent and unhealthy position to women. Women took leading parts in the mystery religions. The cult of the fertility goddess, the *bona dea* in Rome, was restricted to women only and drew down much suspicion of debauchery from the satirists. It was the same with the Bacchanalia, and the cult of Isis. Women had it all their own way in these orgiastic cults, and much public odium resulted. The greatest scandal of all occurred in A.D. 19. The victim was a certain Paulina. She was young, beautiful and blue-blooded, and she had rejected the advances of an equestrian, Decius Mundus, whereupon he bribed the priest of Isis to tell her that the god Anubis wished to spend the night with her in the temple. Needless to say, young Decius stood in for the absent god! This caused a furore in Rome. Tiberius held an enquiry. The priests of Isis were crucified, and Isis worshippers were among four thousand persons immediately deported to Sardinia.

In Corinth itself there was a great temple to Aphrodite the Prostitute on the Acrocorinth, and a thousand prostitutes operated there in service of the goddess of love. We know a good deal about ancient prostitutes, and they were no more difficult to recognise then than in the modern world. Their faces were heavily made up, and they wore no bands in their hair, no veils, and a short, brightly coloured tunic instead of the normal long garment of the Roman matron.

Such, then, was the background. There was little opportunity for a woman to distinguish herself in the ancient world – except by notoriety.

THE JESUS REVOLUTION

Xenophon in the *Oeconomicus* (7f.) gives a delightful cameo of the normal position of women. Isomachus is explaining to Socrates why his bride of fifteen years needs instruction in running the house. 'She had spent the preceding part of her life under the strictest restraint, in order that she might see as little, hear as little and ask as few questions as possible.' It is utterly unlike that in the gospels, particularly the Gospel of Luke. Here we meet Mary the mother of Jesus (Luke 1:26–56), Elizabeth (Luke 1:24f.), Anna the prophetess (Luke 2:36–8), the widow of Nain (Luke 7:11 –17), the woman in the house of Simon who washed Jesus' feet with her tears (Luke 7:36–50), Mary Magdalene from whom Jesus cast out seven demons (Luke 8:2), the society ladies Susanna and Joanna from court who accompanied him around (Luke 8:2), the woman with the issue of blood (Luke 8:42–8), Martha and Mary (Luke 10:38–42), the widow with the two mites (Luke 21:1–4), the weeping daughters of Jerusalem (Luke 23:27–31), and the women gathered round the cross, faithful to the last (Luke 23:49).

Women became the first witnesses of the resurrection when they came to perform the last rites on his body (Luke 24:1f.). Jesus revealed himself first after his resurrection to Mary, outside the tomb (John 20:1f.). The women joined in prayer and supplication with the twelve (Acts 1:14). They helped elect Matthias (Acts 1:15–26), and received the power and gifts of the Holy Spirit on the Day of Pentecost (Acts 2:1f.). The home of Mary, the mother of John Mark, became the headquarters of the earliest church (Acts 12:12). Paul's first convert in Europe was a woman, Lydia (Acts 16:14). Priscilla, who in more than half the references in the New Testament is mentioned before her husband Aquila, joined with him in instructing Apollos (Acts 18:26). We find women engaged in Christian work; women like Mary, Tryphaena and Tryphosa who 'worked hard in the Lord' (Rom. 16:6, 12). We find them associating with Paul in spreading the gospel (Phil. 4:3). We find them assisting in leadership through the two roles of deaconess and widow, both clearly defined in the ancient church (1 Tim. 5:3f., 9–17, 3:8–13, Pliny *Ep.* 10:96). Phoebe was one of those deaconesses, and was clearly a woman of substance and influence since she is called 'patroness' of the church at Cenchreae, which was just down the road from Corinth (Rom. 16:1). As such she would undoubtedly have had some role in worship. As we have seen, Paul was happy for women both to pray and to utter prophecies during public worship (1 Cor. 11:5), and the four prophesying daughters of Philip the evangelist became celebrated in the church (Acts 21:9). To be sure, there were dangers. The church at Thyatira was plagued by a woman with prophetic pretensions who led the people astray: she was like the Old Testament Jezebel, seeking to unite the worship of the Lord with pagan cults (Rev. 2:20). This sort of person was a great embarrassment to the Christian cause. Very bad publicity, and just what Paul was anxious to avoid at Corinth!

THE POSITION OF WOMEN
Paul is abundantly clear on the position of women. 'There is neither Jew nor Greek, there is neither slave nor free, there is neither male nor female: for you are all one in Christ Jesus' (Gal. 3:28). That is fundamental to him. Men and women have complete equality of standing before God. The revolutionary teaching of Jesus had thoroughly percolated into the conservative heart of Paul the rabbi.

He expresses this equality in a beautiful way in 1 Cor.

11:11, 'In the Lord woman is not independent of man nor man of woman; for as woman was made from man, so man is now born from woman.' Thus each owes their existence to the other and cannot do without the other.

But what of all Paul's teaching on the submission of the woman to the man in marriage? Well, it is much misunderstood.

Let us begin with 1 Cor. 11:13. 'I want you to understand that the head of every man is Christ, the head of a woman (*gunē* is used in Greek both for 'wife' and 'woman' – hence some of the confusion in understanding Paul!) is her husband, and the head of Christ is God.' Paul is making a profound statement. There is a deep parallel between the husband–wife relationship and the mankind – Christ relationship. In both there is equality of life: in both there is differentiation of function. Christ is 'head' over man: the husband is 'head' over his wife. There is nothing derogatory about this idea of the headship of the husband: it is strictly parallel to Christ's headship over man, and God's over Christ. In each of the three relationships there is shared life and differing roles.

He takes this matter further, and illuminates it most helpfully in Eph. 5:21f. There he marvellously interweaves the relation between Christ and the church and husband and wife. And it is all in the context of this much-hated word (to our twentieth century ears) of 'subjection'. 'Be subject,' says Paul. 'Take your God-given place.' But notice what he does *not* say. He does not tell the wife to be subject to her husband willy-nilly. He tells them both to be subject to one another. 'Be subject to one another out of reverence for Christ,' he says. And then he begins to spell out what that mutual submission will mean in practice. For the wife this submission will mean three things. She will defer to her husband as she would to the Lord (Eph. 5:22, 24). She will cleave to him as she would to the Lord (Eph. 5:31). And she will respect him as she would the Lord (Eph. 5:33). But if this is to be the proper attitude in the wife, the husband, like Christ, must merit it. He, too, must subordinate his own desires for the sake of his wife. The form his submission takes is different, but just as costly. He must protect his wife, just as Christ would 'save' or 'protect' his spouse, the church (Eph. 5:23). He must sacrifice himself for her, as Christ did for us (Eph. 5:25). And he must cherish her as his own body: that is what Christ does with his body and bride, the church (Eph. 5:29). It is only to such loving self-sacrifice that the wife is bidden to submit. Surrender to self-giving love is not painful; and only self-giving love merits anything of the sort.

It should be clear from all this that Paul has the highest possible view of marriage and the deepest respect for women. He cannot legitimately be charged with anti-feminism. He was no male chauvinist pig. In his view, the wife is to the husband as the church is to Christ; his bride, his very body. Equally, he was clear that in the family it was the task of the husband to undertake overall responsibility and leadership (1 Cor. 11:3, Eph. 5:22). This was no value judgment. He knows men and women are equal as individuals, regardless of their sex. But he was no less sure that they are called to a different function within the marriage bond. The normal place for the wife was not in the pulpit but in the home (1 Tim. 2:11–15). Yet it was through the wives gossiping the gospel in the home, at the laundry, and to friends, just as much as through formal preaching by the husbands, that the Christian faith spread throughout the world.

THE DIFFICULT PASSAGES
What, however, are we to make of two very dismissive passages on the woman's – or rather the wife's – role in teaching? They come in 1 Cor. 14:33–5 and 1 Tim. 2:11–15. They need to be examined with some care, since so much is read into them.

'As in all the churches of the saints, the women should keep silence in the churches. For they are not permitted to speak, but should be subordinate, as even the law says. If there is anything they desire to know, let them ask their husbands at home. For it is shameful for a woman to speak in church, (1 Cor. 14:34–5). [1] At first sight this looks very negative. Nevertheless in this instance it cannot possibly be taken at first sight! The law never enjoins silence on women, and Paul has already permitted women not only to pray aloud but also to prophesy in church (1 Cor. 11:5). They are not restricted to a passive role in worship. They may take a leading, speaking part. How do we reconcile these two passages in the same letter? It is not very difficult. The word Paul uses for 'speak', *lalein*, has been employed a good deal in this chapter for 'to speak in tongues'. It may be that he is here discouraging women from undisciplined and indiscriminate speaking in tongues during the services, and so causing disorder. But it is not necessary so to construe it. Their assemblies were on any showing chaotic. It would not help for the wives to make a lot of disturbance in them by asking endless questions of their husbands: remember that the women of those days received no education, so would naturally want to ask more questions than men would. Let them not chatter away in church (*lalein* is often used for informal chattering) but let them ask any questions of their husbands when they return home. This injunction is perfectly compatible with allowing a woman to pray or prophesy or take some other leading part in the meeting.

Much the more difficult passage is contained in 1 Tim. 2:11f. There, Paul seems to be saying that a woman must 'learn in silence with all submissiveness'. He permits 'no woman to teach or to have authority over (*authentein*) men; she is to keep silent.' He bases this on the priority of Adam's creation over Eve's, and the fact that Eve was deceived by the serpent while Adam was not deceived – simply disobedient. The role he sees for women is childbearing, faith, love and holiness with modesty.

On any showing Paul does not want women to establish norms of doctrine in the church. But is she never to teach in

[1] *Gunē* can mean 'woman' or 'wife'. Here the context is unambiguous. Paul is forbidding wives to chatter in the assembly, not women as such to speak.

mixed company? That would be a little strange in view of the women like Lydia, Euodia, Tryphaena, and Phoebe, who laboured in the gospel and presumably were not always totally insulated from the male ear . . .

A fascinating piece of research has been done in recent years on the meaning of the word *authentein*, normally translated 'exercise authority over'. It occurs nowhere else in the New Testament. It is clearly a key word in this passage, however, and this passage plays a key role in the supposedly scriptural argument that a woman should always keep silent in mixed company. C. C. Kroeger shows convincingly that *authentein* did not have the meaning of 'bear rule' in New Testament times. The main background of the word, in Euripides, Philodemus and Phrynicus is erotic. The same is true in Wisd. 12:6. It has strong sexual overtones, and St John Chrysostom is probably right in understanding it in his *Commentary* on 1 Timothy to mean 'sexual licence'.

This, of course, utterly alters the meaning of the passage. Paul is saying that he does not allow a woman to teach men obscenity and fornication. This was a serious problem in the ancient church, with all the female-based fertility cults which came over from paganism. The Thyatiran Jezebel taught Christians to practice immorality (Rev. 2:20, cf. Num. 25:3, 31:15f., and see 2 Pet. 2:14f., 18, together with 2 Tim. 3:6f.). Licentious doctrines played an enormous part in the gnosticism which was even then beginning to invade the church, and Clement of Alexandria in the second century, whilst complaining of those who turn the love-feasts into orgies, uses this very word *authentēs* (*Strom*. 3:18).

This interpretation would make excellent sense of the whole passage. Women are told to dress modestly in a city where there were many courtesans (1 Tim. 2:9–11). 'Silence' would indicate learning Christian doctrine quietly, in subjection to the gospel. In Ephesus, where many sacred prostitutes were attached to the shrine of Diana, worshippers were taught that fornication brought them into close union with the deity (and both the Gnostics and the Nestorians used the *authentein* root to justify this). But converts must learn that there is one God and only one mediator between God and man, the man Christ Jesus (1 Tim. 2:5). They must practise their faith in quiet decorum, not with the orgies demanded by Ephesian religion. Moreover, the devil had once deceived Eve (the verb 'deceive' used in 1 Tim. 2:14 also has sexual overtones); and to women, many of whom had been involved in the immoralities of the Phrygian cult, the admonition Paul gives was certainly appropriate. Virtually without exception women teachers in Greek society were *hetairai*, courtesans, and made it evident in the course of their lectures that they would be available afterwards. But the Book of Proverbs had made it plain that to seduce men in this way is to lead them to slaughter (Prov. 2:18, 5:5, 7:27) and murder is the other of the ancient meanings of *authentein*: in this rare word the erotic and the murderous combine. 'Saved' through childbirth (2 Tim. 2:15) might refer to the social and economic salvation or rescue of the woman through marriage and the family. Or it might reflect a proper Christian concern for the illegitimate children brought into the world through immoral practices: in the mention of this word *authentein* in the Wisdom of Solomon it refers to 'parents engendering helpless souls'. Maybe Paul, who knew and quoted Wisdom, caught the allusion and was moved to reflect that the gospel of the Saviour could rescue not only the mother from immorality but the child from the stigma of illegitimacy. Both personalities could be healed; and faith, love, holiness with self-control would grow in those who were once the women of the streets.

I do not know that this interpretation of a difficult passage can be proved. But it makes sense. It does justice to the Greek, to the whole context, to the thought of Paul, to the power of the gospel, and to the meretricious background both of Corinth and Ephesus. And it removes the glaring inconsistency from an apostle who clearly did use women in ministry and yet in this passage appears to deny them any lot or part in it. If this interpretation is even a serious possibility (and it is), it ought to loosen up a great many of the restrictive attitudes on the subject which are found in circles of Christians who genuinely want to find out what the Bible teaches and be guided by it. At least it will make us think again, and perhaps help to ensure that Christianity, which was in the van of women's liberation in the first century, is not one of the last bodies in the world of the twentieth century to allow women a significant place in leadership.

THE PLACE OF WOMEN IN MINISTRY

In the light of all this, how are we to assess the proper place of women in ministry? On the one hand we have to recognise their total equality with men in the sight of God and in the Body of Christ. On the other, we have to give due weight to the supportive role which is always theirs, even in the New Testament. There are no women apostles, no women presbyters: there are women helpers, women deacons, women prophets.

Should women, then, be ordained?

I believe this is the wrong question, because we have got ordination all wrong. Professor Alan Richardson saw this clearly. 'To admit women to the priesthood would leave the present unsatisfactory situation exactly where it is, and would do nothing to promote the development of a wide variety of ministries, which is the church's most immediate need' (*Women and Holy Orders* p. 126). Developments since he wrote only confirm his fears. Churches which have enthusiastically ordained women priests find it very hard to place them. The fact is that all Christians are called to minister, all without exception. Women as well as men may receive the *charisma* of leadership. I do not see why the church should not appropriately recognise this by ordination. But remember that presbyters are always plural in the New Testament. It is when we go for leadership by one person that we fall into difficulties. So it is wise for both men and women always to operate in a *fellowship of leadership*. The women would not be over the men in such a team, but alongside them. The creation pattern could best be retained if the chairmanship of a mixed team were normally in the hands of a man.[1] It would also give plenty of room for the full emergence and development of the undoubted gifts of leadership which women possess; gifts which Paul both recognised and utilised. So long as ministry is seen to be the calling of all Christians; so long as ordination is reformed and seen as the recognition by the church of the God-given *charisma* of leadership, bestowed by him on some members of his Body in the local church for the benefit of all members – then there seems to me to be no biblical or rational obstacle to women taking their full place in such a team.

And if all this seems very futuristic, it need not be so at all. In our own church women form part of the full-time team alongside men. Women as well as men may occupy the role of 'lay pastor' within our congregation. To be sure, they are not ordained. They are not priests, or presbyters, in the eyes of the Church of England. That could not be until the church as a whole has decided how and when to act on female ordinations. But they are sharing with men in the work of ministry within the congregation. And they are universally recognised by that congregation whom they see themselves privileged to serve. In their pastoral role they do sometimes have oversight over men: as did women of the calibre of Priscilla and Phoebe in the first century, and women missionaries for a hundred years and more. We have seen from a careful examination of this passage in 1 Timothy 2, that Paul does nothing to forbid it. Accordingly women in our congregation lead groups, lead dance and drama in worship, preach, lead the prayers of the congregation, contribute in a prophetic role within the church from time to time, assist in administering the Holy Communion, share in a healing prayer group for the sick, proclaim the

[1] The concept of 'headship' is improperly introduced into this discussion. Paul teaches it is the husband who is 'head' over his wife, not man as such over woman as such in the church.

gospel and teach the faith. The only thing a woman does not do in our congregation is to celebrate the eucharist; no man does either, unless he is ordained. That is a domestic ordinance of the Church of England. Until and unless it is changed the headship of any ministerial team must lie with an ordained man. The man without the woman however, is incomplete. This we recognise, and act accordingly. So did Paul, although both by reason of expediency in volatile Corinth and by conviction from Genesis[1] he kept the presidency of the ministry team in the hands of man. I *think* he would if he were alive today: I am not sure. But I am certain that he would be appalled to see how small a part in leadership the modern church gives to women, and amazed, too, to see how grossly he had been misunderstood!

---

[1] It may well be that in the throes of newly-discovered brotherhood and sisterhood in Christ there was a danger of home relationships being overwhelmed. Perhaps this is why Paul was at pains to reinforce his pleas for a certain subjection of wives to husbands by appealing to Gen. 3:16. This was a matter of social order, not of spiritual equality. On that, as we have seen, Paul stood firm as a rock. In Christ there could be no 'male or female'. He has been berated for failing to move from the recognition of this principle to its immediate application in the church; unfairly, it seems to me. It would have been untimely. He had also perceived that in Christ 'there can be no bond or free', and yet he had sent the slave Onesimus back to his master Philemon (Philem. 12). In each case he supported existing customs for the time being, while enunciating principles which would in due course utterly abolish them.

CHAPTER SEVENTEEN

APOSTLES

It is almost no exaggeration to say that the Corinthian correspondence hinges round the question of the true and the false apostle. As this is a fundamental issue, I have delayed consideration of it to the final chapter.

It affects Christian teaching. How far, for instance, is variety in doctrine acceptable? Are there any norms for what Christians teach?

It affects Christian unity. What is authentically Christian? How shall we assess the rival claims of independency, presbytery, episcopacy? More important still, is the church sacerdotal? Must it be an institution? Is there a particular form which is integral to any expression of the true church, or is freedom from form a mark of genuineness?

The question of apostleship takes us to the heart of Christianity. And what these letters have to tell us is paradoxical stuff, in all conscience. In 1 Cor. 1:1 Paul maintains robustly that he is one of the apostles. In 1 Cor. 12:28 he maintains that they are 'first' in the church. Yet in 1 Cor. 4:9 they are the last in the gladiatorial show.

WHAT IS AN APOSTLE?
You have only to consider the use made of 'apostle' in the Roman Catholic Church on the one hand and the house-

church movement on the other, to realise that this is a highly contemporary question. It is one which has been much discussed in learned circles in recent years by such scholars as Rengstorff, Geldenhuys, Schweizer, Friedrichsen, von Campenhausen and Hahn.

The term is used only twice in St Mark, the oldest Gospel. In Mark 3.14f. it is applied to the twelve apostles, whose function is to be with Jesus and then to be sent forth to teach. The Gospel shows them fulfilling both these roles. Then in Mark 6:30 they are called 'apostles' when they return from the mission on which Jesus had sent them. St Matthew also restricts the term 'apostles' to their mission journey (Matt. 10:2, 5). St Luke's references are a little more plentiful, showing that Jesus chose the apostles from a much larger circle of disciples (Luke 6:13), calling them 'apostles' on their mission journey as in Matthew and Mark (Luke 9:10). They would ask for an increased measure of faith so that they could effectively carry out the programme of Jesus (Luke 17:5). At the solemn moment of the Last Supper the twelve are designated as apostles (Luke 22:14) as they are when they receive tidings of the resurrection (Luke 24:10). The fourth Gospel does not use the title for the twelve at all, but much of the book is concerned to show how Jesus prepared them for their future mission by being with him: the Holy Spirit would later equip them to carry out his work (John 13:16, 14:25f., 16:12–14).

They are 'disciples' or learners, then, during the ministry, designated as 'apostles' or 'delegates' only on their trial run in mission and when seen by Luke as anticipating the messianic gospel and the messianic banquet. But after the resurrection they are called to be witnesses to Jesus (Acts 1:8, Luke 24:48, John 20:21f.), given understanding of the scriptures (Luke 24:45) and equipped with his Spirit (Acts 1:8, John 20:22). They are the group which will found the universal church.

The key idea in all this is the Jewish *shaliach*, the one sent with his master's authority in his master's name. The rabbis had a saying, 'He who is sent is as him who sends him,' and this concept underlies the repeated command of Jesus, 'As the Father has sent me, even so I send you' (John 20:21). The apostle is as his Lord. He is the representative of Jesus, equipped with Jesus' power and authority. It is clear from the Gospels that Jesus anticipated a world mission for the apostolic circle. The Acts of the Apostles shows how it happened.

WHO ARE APOSTLES?
Did the early church see only the twelve in this cardinal role as apostles? Or was it wider? The answer seems to be that there were two understandings of 'apostle'. One is restricted to the apostle of Jesus Christ. The other is the 'apostle of the churches': in other words, the delegate of the church sent out for a specific role. The term is used in 2 Cor. 8:23 and Phil. 2:25 in this way. The Jerusalem church certainly had emissaries with this title, delegates from the church at large (Gal. 2:12, 2 Cor. 10:12–15, 11:5 and 13). Possibly 'apostles' is used in this wide sense in 1 Cor. 15:7, and in all probability Luke sees Paul and Barnabas as apostles in this secondary, derived sense in Acts 14:4, 14. For he only calls them 'apostles' when they are emissaries of the Antioch church engaged on the specific task of the First Missionary Journey.

Apart, however, from this secondary use of apostle as delegate of the church for a specific function, the word has a very restricted and particular usage in the New Testament. It is applied to the twelve and Paul; perhaps to James (Gal. 1:19) and Barnabas (1 Cor. 9:5, 6) and, even more improbably, Andronicus and Junias (Rom. 16:7). It denoted a small but identifiable band, the contemporaries, friends and emissaries of Jesus, to which Paul could be considered a late addition (1 Cor. 15:8). Paul is passionately convinced that he is a member of this select club, but others manifestly disagreed, so he had to be very clear on what it involved.

There are five qualifications which Paul mentions in these letters.

1. A personal commissioning by God (1 Cor. 1:1).

2. An encounter with the risen Lord (1 Cor. 9:1, 15:7). This would account for James' inclusion in the apostolic ranks if Gal. 1:19 should be construed inclusively: before the resurrection he was not even a believer (John 7:5).

3. A travelling, supervisory role over the local churches (1 Cor. 9:1f., 2 Cor. 13:1–3, cf. Acts 14:23).

4. A foundation role for the church of Christ (1 Cor. 12:28, Eph. 2:20, Rev. 21:14, 2 Cor. 10:8). Apostles were the living embodiment of the continuity between the Jesus of history and the Christ of faith. They could not be evaded or sidestepped. There was – and is – no independent access to Jesus Christ except through them. They belong to the age of the incarnation just as much as to the age of the church.

5. An authority like Christ's (2 Cor. 13:10) and a lifestyle like Christ's in holiness, in suffering and in power (1 Cor. 4:9, 2 Cor. 4:7–10, 13:1–4, 10).

WHAT ARE THE MARKS OF THE TRUE APOSTLE?
As we have seen there were others around in the early church who made use of that title: some of them 'apostles of the churches' living unworthily, others claiming to be among the small circle of 'apostles of Christ' but denying it by their lives and lips. Such were false apostles, Satan's apostles (2 Cor. 11:13), dangerous men. How, according to Paul, could they be distinguished?

First, false apostles are showy people boasting worldly things (2 Cor. 11:22f., 10:2–4, 5:16). This worldliness showed up in a number of ways. They claimed to have known Jesus personally (2 Cor. 5:16). They laid a great stress on their Hebrew lineage and pedigree (2 Cor. 11:21f.). They flaunted letters of commendation to their charges (2 Cor. 3:1). Boasting had replaced selflessness in these 'superlative apostles' (2 Cor. 11:5).

Second, these false apostles were destructive people pulling the church apart. This is apparent from the whole vitriolic campaign at Corinth against Paul, coupled with his repeated assertions that his authority was given him by the

Lord for building up, not pulling down (2 Cor. 10:8, 13:10).

Third, these false apostles were superior people who were quick to avoid sacrifice. This is apparent from 2 Cor. 11:23f., 11:5, 12 and Paul's description of the hardships of the true apostle in 1 Cor. 4:9f.

Reliance on status, division of churches, and avoidance of the way of the cross are still high among the marks of the false apostle today. These false apostles pandered to the Corinthians' worldly ideas of leadership – rhetorical, charging big fees, bombastic about their qualifications, contemptuous of others, overbearing. This was typical of the Greek peripatetic teachers, and it was this concept of apostles that Paul was attacking in 1 Cor. 1–4. Now in 2 Cor. 3–6 and 10–13 the issue reaches its climax. It is the question of the true and the false apostle. The true apostle demonstrates authentic Christianity (which is why Paul is so vehement in his defence. He, as an apostle, speaks for his Master). The type of Christian leader favoured by the Corinthians, on the other hand, is the embodiment of this world and its ruler. Would they put his apostleship to the test? He gives three immediate criteria.

First, they themselves are the proof of his apostleship. So far from needing written commendations, 'you yourselves are our letter of recommendation, written on your hearts, to be known and read by all men' (2 Cor. 3:2). They themselves and their conversion to Christ constituted the seal of his apostleship (1 Cor. 9:2).

Second, Paul's power in and through the Holy Spirit underlined his claims to be a true apostle. He is very clear that there are such things as 'signs of a true apostle' (2 Cor. 12:12) and they include 'patience, with signs and wonders and mighty works'. In the apostle, men have to do with the living embodiment of the powerful Jesus Christ (2 Cor. 13:3). 'He who is sent is as him who sent him . . .'

Third, true apostles show themselves by their suffering. The Corinthians were infected by a theology of glory. Paul has to remind them of the centrality of the cross (1 Cor. 2:2). The apostle is as his Lord: he too has to tread the way of suffering, humiliation, weakness and death. Corinthian teaching about the kingdom of God, like that of many enthusiastic and charismatic groups since then, seems to have embodied an almost completely realised eschatology. They were already revelling in the powers of the age to come. They had already entered into their reign! To all this Paul says a resounding 'No'. Eschatology is inaugurated, not realised. The last days have begun, but are not yet completed. The powers of the age to come have been tasted, not quaffed. This side of death all Christians, not least apostles, are called to identify with a suffering Messiah. That is the meaning of 1 Cor. 4:8–13, of 2 Cor. 4:7–12 of 2 Cor. 11:21–30. The path of the cross must match the power of the resurrection in the true apostle of Jesus Christ.

WHAT IS THE SIGNIFICANCE OF THE APOSTLES?
They are historically unique, and doctrinally normative. Historically unique, because you cannot have more than one bottom storey to a building. These men bridge the gap between the Jesus who walked this earth and the Christ who reigns in glory. They afford a continuity to balance the discontinuity of the ascension. They are the companions of Jesus, the guarantors of the continuity between the Lord then and now, the witnesses of the resurrection. Their place is unique and unrepeatable. That is why they did not appoint other apostles in their place. Like any *shaliach* their authority returned to the sender. It was not in principle something that could be further delegated. Instead of apostles they seem to have appointed bishop-presbyters or bishops, presbyters and deacons instead. They are unique.

Not only so, they are decisive for the faith of the church. All through history God had revealed himself through event and interpretation. When he came to embody his message in person (Heb. 1:1f.) it is hardly surprising that the disciples often failed to understand. So he promised that the Spirit would guide them in their interpretation of him to future generations (John 16:12–14). The Holy Spirit would enable them to understand and interpret the greatest event in history – the person and significance of Jesus Christ. That is why the apostles were so important in the early church. Like the prophets, they were bearers of revelation (Eph. 2:20, Rev. 21:14). The Acts of the Apostles gives the flavour. The people did not dare to join them, but held them in high honour (Acts 5:13). The fellowship and authorised teaching of the church embodies their fellowship and teaching (Acts 2:42). It is they who appoint elders (Acts 14:23), decide policy (Acts 15:23f.) and administer property (Acts 4:35). They are the Lord's representatives, and his executors in judgment also, as the stories of Ananias and Sapphira and Elymas show (Acts 5:1–11, 13:10f.).

This is the authority which Paul claimed as latecomer to the apostolic family. When that authority is accepted he writes like a father (1 Cor. 4:15). When it is scouted, he writes as a judge (2 Cor. 13:1f.). In the apostle men have to do with the indwelling Christ. And he continues his teaching role through them. This is what Jesus foresaw for them. This is what they themselves claimed (see Gal. 1:6–12, 1 Thess. 2:13, 2 John 10, 1 Pet. 1:11–12, Rev. 22:18f.). And this is what the subsequent church understood both by closing the canon and also by their express statements. Thus Clement, writing from Rome about A.D. 95 says, 'Christ is from God and the apostles from Christ' (Ep. 42). Ignatius, his contemporary, writes, 'I do not command you like Peter and Paul. They were apostles' (Romans 4), and in a famous passage in Philadelphians 5 he puts the prophets, the apostles and the gospel on the same authoritative level. Bishop Serapion of Antioch wrote about A.D. 180, 'We accept the apostles as the Lord himself.' That attitude was characteristic of the early Christians. The apostles were decisive for the faith of the church. What could not be shown to derive from apostolic circles was not to be imposed on any Christian as necessary belief. The apostles were the norms of doctrine.

WHAT IS THE SUCCESSION TO THE APOSTLES?

There are three ways in which this question can be answered. Looked at from one point of view there are and there can be no successors of the apostles. They did not appoint any, and the whole essence of apostleship is that they are authoritative representatives of Jesus, but cannot pass that role on to others. One who is a delegate cannot delegate his powers. The apostles shared, in some way, in the uniqueness and particularity of the incarnation.

Looked at from another point of view, the apostles have a succession – in their doctrine. This teaching was, as we have seen, decisive for the church of the first century, and it remains so throughout history. If you want to know what Christianity is and teaches, you must turn to the apostles and their colleagues. There is nowhere else. When the doctrine of 'apostolic succession' began at the end of the second century A.D. it was not a question of a succession of hands imposed on the bishop; it was succession in office in order to safeguard the true teaching of the apostles over against those who claimed a hidden *gnōsis*. C. H. Turner has made that abundantly plain in his 'Apostolic Succession – the original concept' in *Essays on the Early History of the Church and Ministry*. Apostolic succession, then, is to be found in the scriptures that they wrote.

Viewed from a third perspective, there is a succession to the apostles in their supervisory role. In the earliest church there was a settled local ministry of presbyters, and a circulating supervisory ministry of apostles and apostolic men like Titus, Timothy, Silas and Mark. Clement of Alexandria tells us that in his old age John set up bishops in the Roman province of Asia in order to provide precisely this circulating ministry of oversight that the apostles had offered. The story is probably true. Certainly in the second century monepiscopacy (oversight by one man) is well nigh universal, and it would be hard to imagine this unless one of the apostles had in fact inaugurated it. The value of a 'pastor for the pastors' is too obvious to need emphasis, and the majority of Christendom has made good use of it until the present day. The bishop is a symbol of the catholicity of the church across the world and down the years. It is only when he sees himself as a successor of the apostles in terms of doctrine and ultimate authority that Christians have a right to object.

WHAT IS A CHURCH THAT IS APOSTOLIC?

There is some ambivalence when we try to answer that question about a church; it is an ambivalence inherent in the apostle himself.

Thus Paul could not prove his apostleship. He was approved by the 'pillar' apostles at Jerusalem (Gal. 2:9) and yet he had hardly gone back to Antioch when one 'pillar' rebuked another (Gal. 2:11–12). To be sure, Paul had the proof of his converts, yet, as the Corinthian correspondence shows, at times even they seemed reprobate (2 Cor. 13:5). He had conviction, but no palpable proof. His life and death were the demonstration of his claims.

It was the same with Jesus. When challenged to give a compelling sign that he was sent by the Father he was not able to produce one. His life and death were the only lasting demonstration of his claims.

It is hardly likely to be otherwise with the apostolic character of the church. If we search for infallible marks, we shall fail to find them. There is no order that can guarantee life, no orthodoxy that can guarantee vitality.

This does not mean that anything goes. That would be far from the truth. Let us look at what makes a church apostolic, first negatively and then positively.

1. *A church is not apostolic if it is narrowly exclusive.* 'Welcome one another . . . as Christ has welcomed you' is the injunction of Rom. 15:7.

2. *A church is not apostolic if it fails to administer discipline.* Persistent sin must be dealt with. Paul is quite clear about this in 1 Cor. 5:1, but even so he is anxious that the man shall be restored as soon as he is penitent (1 Cor. 5:5).

3. *A church is not apostolic if it fails to care for the needy.*

Paul's concern for the minority poor in Jerusalem (2 Cor. 8 and 9) is a notable example of this compassion which so marked the ministry of Jesus. There is plenty of middle-class captivity of the church in Britain, isolationism in the churches of the U.S.A., and terrible social indifference and injustice in the Catholicism of Latin America. These things make a mockery of any claim to follow the apostles.

4. *A church is not apostolic if it shrinks from mission*. Whatever its credentials, it cannot claim to be apostolic if it has ceased to go out like the apostles to reach men with the gospel. 'As the Father has sent me, so send I you' is an essential mark of a church which is apostolic.

5. *A church is not apostolic if it needlessly splits off from others*. The appalling tendency to schism (often for trifling causes) among some of the newer churches in many parts of the world has nothing in common with apostolic Christianity. The apostles made herculean efforts to keep the church together, with mutual recognition and respect despite the variety of worship and customs. They knew they were one body in Christ, and that went for Jew, Samaritan or Gentile. There could so easily have been three denominations at the very outset of the church's mission, yet they resolutely set their faces against any such thing, as Acts records. How can a church demonstrate the reconciling work of Christ when it is unreconciled with other branches?

So much for the negative indicators; now for the positive.

1. *An apostolic church concentrates on the person and work of the Lord Jesus Christ* (1 Cor. 3:22f.). Ministers are 'fathers', seeking to bring Christ to birth in people (1 Cor. 4:14f.), and then seeking the maturity of their charges (1 Cor. 2:6f.). Christ-centredness is the essence of a church that is apostolic.

2. *An apostolic church is governed by the teaching of the Lord Jesus Christ*. It honours and respects his teaching. It seeks to be governed by it and abide by it, not to water it down, pare it away, or maintain that it does not mean what it says.

3. *An apostolic church executes the mission of the Lord*

Jesus Christ. It goes out into the world not only to tell the truth but to embody it. It sets out to love people, to win them, to build them up into an outpost of the kingdom of God.

4. *An apostolic church believes in and claims the power of the Lord Jesus Christ.* His Spirit is present, and the power of that Spirit is experienced in faith and expectancy (1 Cor. 4:20, 2 Cor. 4:10, 12:12, 13:4). His risen life is in every apostolic church; and if a church shows none of that 'power of the age to come', then it is not apostolic, however ancient its pedigree.

5. *An apostolic church carries about the dying of the Lord Jesus.* There is nothing triumphalist about such a church, nothing arrogant. It has an authenticity that comes from suffering, from identifying with the poor, and from enduring mockery and persecution. Who can deny that the suffering churches of China and Russia are apostolic whether or not their leadership is episcopal? Like the Master himself, they are not concerned with glory, but submit to suffering. The dying of the Lord Jesus is reflected in their individual and congregational lives. The cross figures in at least three ways in such a church:

in its daily life (2 Cor. 4:7–12).

in its message (1 Cor. 2:2–5).

in its weakness and exposure (1 Cor. 4:8–13).

If an individual fails to meet these requirements he will show himself to be heir to the false apostles denounced in these letters, whose lips proclaimed one message and whose lives another. People will not be drawn to Christ through such a medium.

If a church fails to meet these requirements it will fail to embody the mission of Jesus Christ; it will not exercise any lasting impact for his kingdom.

And if a whole denomination fails to meet these requirements, God may have to decline to use that denomination. It has happened in the past, and will doubtless happen again. Denominations have no divine right to survive, even if they are looking to Paul, Apollos, or Peter as their founder. God will not share his glory with leaders of a denomination. If churches want denominational glory they are welcome to it. But they will not display the beauty or demonstrate the power of Jesus Christ.

These are humbling reflections. We are far too prone to see apostleship as something that belongs to us; something we have all the time, if we have it at all. Alas, it is far more frail, far less adhesive than that. It is not so much a status; more a way of life. We need constantly, as Paul exhorted the Corinthians, to examine ourselves, and check up on our discipleship. Otherwise for all our preaching to others we may ourselves be castaways, for all our talk about discipleship we may prove to be reprobates. If it could happen at Corinth it can happen at Canterbury, Rome or Geneva. Let him who thinks he stands, Paul warned the Corinthians, take heed lest he fall.

We are not called to constant success. We are not called to instant glory now. We live between the ages; heirs to all the failure and frailty and fallenness of this age, heirs too to the power and life and love of the age to come. We live at the cross roads. The Master suffered . . . and rose. So will his apostolic church, and only that.